Trained by the world's best healers, Michael is brilliant, sensitive and highly conscious. Best of all, he knows how to make me feel safe. I've been on a healing journey from a troubled childhood for literally 50 years. I've had therapy, both traditional and holistic, from the "BEST of the BEST." No one, in all that line of gifted and brilliant healers has done more for me than the author of this remarkable book. My experience with Michael has been both life-changing and soul-nourishing. If you are committed to your Soul Growth, Michael is the person to assist you!

Linda Schiller-Hanna - Clairvoyant, Counselor, Lecturer, Intuition Trainer - USA, ARE - Association for Research and Enlightenment - Edgar Cayce Foundation

A truly sensitive and insightful piece of work written from the heart by a caring and dedicated human being who is committed to learning about his spiritual origins, and by doing so is learning about the totality of who he is. A book everyone should read irrespective of whether they are interested in discovering their Spirit Selves, already walking their own path to enlightenment or just darn right inquisitive.

Elizabeth Francis - Spiritual Teacher, Psychic, Author - England

I've had the privilege of knowing and working with Michael since 1983. If you want to improve your life; heal; grow spiritually; or if your life isn't working, then Michael is the person to go to. One session may provide the answers you have been seeking. I've been counseling for 35 years, but only Michael can hit it right on the head immediately.

Dr. Edith Ann Thomas - Counselor, Psychic, Author - USA

This profound, enriching book is the beautiful present of Michael to humanity. Based on his own true, revealing and intriguing quest, it teaches us an intuitive approach to the healing of the soul's wounds through growth and expansion in consciousness, towards the ultimate goal of Transcendence. I highly recommend it both for seekers and therapists on the path to self-realization.

Avi Hay - Spiritual Teacher, Author - Spain

I love this very well written book. It's a wonderful introduction to what Michael does, and offers excellent examples of how he works. Michael came into our lives ten years ago. He helped my family and me clear many energy and spiritual blockages, and assisted us to 'see' life more clearly. He helped me to open up to energy/spiritual work and nurtured me along my path as a healer. Michael is in the elite realm of mastery in energy/spiritual work - he works at a much higher level than most others. I absolutely recommend Michael for your energy/spiritual needs, awareness, growth and healing.

Denny MacArthur - Educator, Psychic, Search & Rescue - New Zealand

Michael has helped many of my friends, family members and clients. This book is a brilliant piece of work - a spiritual gift! It's the book I have been searching for! It's like opening a treasure chest and saying "Oh Wow!" It will be my guide for many years to come and I hope yours too!

Elspeth Kerr - Spiritual Teacher, Hypnotherapist, Reiki Master, Healer - Cyprus

I've thoroughly enjoyed reading it. Michael has written a brilliant "all time" informative book that will appeal and inform people from all levels of spiritual understanding. I highly recommend it.

Sohani Gonzalez, B.A. - Homeopath, LCH, MCH - England

Your wonderful book provided many "Aha" moments and very helpful insights.

Marni - Nurse for 20 years - USA

Michael is a powerful healer who has positively impacted our family with his knowledge and wisdom. This book synthesizes the key elements of our spiritual journey and the human reality.

Karen Boyes - CEO Spectrum Education - New Zealand

If you are curious about where you came from and why you are on earth, many of your questions may be answered in Bradford's book, which inspires awe and joy, amazement and recognition. Many of us experience soul hunger, a state where we know we are meant for more than working and eating, but too many of us never allow our curiosity to soar in the direction of having a language of spirituality. Michael gifts us with the pitch-perfect ideas and language for soul expansion, which leads to a greater spiritual IQ, a greater peace, a transcendent recognition of our own souls.

Pat Hoppe, M.A. - USA

Michael's vast knowledge is apparent in this comprehensive text charting the course of human experience.

L. Green - Psychic, Bodyworker - USA

Michael offers a manual for awakened living, an extensive overview of collected wisdom for the human journey from the perspective of a highly intuitive healer. From coming into earthly existence, to the soul's lessons and challenges of being human, to near-death, reincarnation and death, Bradford provides insights into manifesting our soul's deepest longings in this human existence. He shares his experiences as a healer and in being healed with many detailed anecdotal stories to illustrate the adventure and the lessons. Highly recommended for those who wish to accelerate their spiritual growth, awareness and healing in this precious life.

Marina Lenny - Yoga Practitioner, Architect, Designer, Real Estate Investor - USA

Mastering The Human Experience:

Your Soul's Journey on Earth

Mastering The Human Experience:
Your Soul's Journey on Earth

Disclaimer:

Michael Bradford is not a medical doctor or a medical practitioner. He does not medically diagnose nor prescribe any treatment. The author and publisher make no representation and assume no responsibility for the accuracy of information contained herein. You are encouraged to confirm any information obtained from or through this book with other sources, and review all information regarding any medical condition or treatment with your physician.

NEVER DISREGARD PROFESSIONAL MEDICAL ADVICE OR DELAY SEEKING MEDICAL TREATMENT BECAUSE OF SOMETHING YOU HAVE READ IN THIS BOOK.

The information and stories presented in this book are not intended or implied to represent that they are used to diagnose, cure, treat or prevent any medical problem or psychological disorder, nor are they intended as a substitute for seeking professional medical advice, diagnosis or treatment. Michael Bradford strongly advises that you seek professional medical advice before making any health decision.

Any information, stories, examples or testimonials presented in this book do not constitute a warranty, guarantee or prediction regarding the outcome of an individual using any material or information contained herein for any particular purpose or issue. All content, including text, graphics, images and information, contained herein is for general information purposes only.

Michael Bradford accepts no responsibility or liability whatsoever for the use or misuse of the information contained in this book.

By reading this book you agree to fully release, indemnify, and hold harmless, Michael Bradford, his heirs, personal representatives, consultants, employees, agents, and assigns from any claim or liability of whatsoever kind or nature which you may incur arising at any time out of or in relation to your use of the information presented in this book. If any court of law rules that any part of the Disclaimer is invalid, the Disclaimer stands as if those parts were struck out.

Dedication

This book is dedicated to all the beings and interactions — both human and non-human — including guides, teachers, healers, friends, partners, clients, students, apprentices, plants, fish, animals and spirits who helped teach me and shape me into the person I am today. I honor the many lands and Earth energies that inspired my spiritual journey.

I am especially grateful to those who challenged me and appeared in my life as my nemeses. All of my life experiences have influenced me, awakened me, honed my skills and polished my rough edges. For all of them, I am eternally grateful.

Preface

It seems like everything is speeding up these days. Technology is advancing faster and faster. Yet we humans are struggling to understand who we are, where we came from, where we fit in and how to deal with our thoughts, feelings, emotions, wants, needs and desires.

In this book, I share with you the information, knowledge, understanding, perspective and wisdom I've gained over my lifetime. My journey has not been one of reading books. It has been about actively seeking out and spending quality time with the very best healers and teachers all over the Earth. I hope this information will provide you with a firm foundation, as well as an overview, to assist you on your spiritual journey here on Earth.

This is the book I wish I was given when I started my spiritual journey. It provides you with the big picture overview perspective as well as many details. I hope it helps you immensely.

As a child, I was very open and hypersensitive. I would sense things, know things and talk about things that often got me into trouble. I would sometimes unintentionally verbalize what others were trying to suppress and hide. For example, when I was about seven years old, I was with my parents and a group of people. Someone's father had recently died but no one was talking about it. Feeling overwhelmed by all the unexpressed emotions and tension in the room, I started talking about fathers and death. I had no conscious knowledge of what I was doing or what was going on; I was simply emotionally receiving, processing and verbalizing the energy in the room.

Growing up empathic, I felt overwhelmed and overloaded by my feelings and emotions. I did not understand them or the intensity with which I felt them. In high school, I focused on what made sense to me, what I felt was tangible and what I could trust and rely on — math and science. I did well in those two subjects.

All my life, I have felt a sense of urgency, as if something was calling, pushing and pulling me, all at the same time. Even as a child, I wanted to help people. In high school, I wanted to be a doctor.

In college, I took chemical engineering as a part of my pre-med studies. However, due to early childhood trauma, I did not have the emotional stability or the financial support to sustain it, so I dropped out after my second year. For the next three years, I worked days as a chemical lab technician and took college courses during the evenings and summers. However I started to feel like my education was taking too long, so I took a full time night shift job as a janitor so that I could return to college full time during the days and summers.

In 1968, at age 24, I graduated with a degree in business. Eleven years later, I received my Master's degree in International Management with a major in Japanese Studies.

In 1977, when I was 33 years old and living in Dallas, Texas, I joined a singles group where I met some people who were spiritually-minded. One day, while talking with a few of the people in this group, one of the women looked at me and said, "You are a healer!" My response was, "What is that?" She answered, "You need to come with us." To which I replied, "Where are we going?"

A month later, I was on an airplane flying from Dallas, Texas to Mazatlan, Mexico where I met three Psychic Surgeons from the Philippines. Each week, groups of people from all over the USA were flying in to have healing sessions. These gifted healers also told me that I was a healer.

They blessed my hands and invited me to work alongside them, and to assist them in the healing rooms. My job was to energetically prepare the people for surgery, to hold the pans during the operations and to energetically smooth out their energy field after the operations. After a few days of assisting, they invited me to stay and to help them for the entire time they were in Mazatlan. I gladly changed my return flight so I could stay longer and learn as much as I could from them. This was a golden opportunity for me to work and learn alongside them. At first, I had little confidence in myself or in my abilities; however, with time and experience my confidence grew.

This, along with many other experiences, awakened something deep inside of me. Since then, I've met and shared healing experiences with many hundreds of very gifted spiritual teachers, energy healers, psychics, channels, shamans, medicine people and highly spiritual people.

I had a hunger for answers, for healing myself, as well as for understanding myself, my feelings, my emotions, my journey and the reasons we are here on Earth. Initially my interest was only in healing myself, in learning and in gaining an understanding of what I was feeling and experiencing. This hunger motivated me to travel all over the world. I never imagined I would ever become a healer or a spiritual teacher.

Over the past 35 years, I've travelled to all 50 states of the U.S.A. and to over 52 countries, meeting and sharing healing experiences with Native American (First Nation) Medicine People, Canadian Medicine People, an Eskimo Healer, Mexican Shamans, Peruvian Shamans, the Maoris in New Zealand and many hundreds of complementary therapists, healers, psychics, channels, shamans and holistic medical professionals.

I have studied Hypnosis (since 1972), Neuro-Linguistic Programming (since 1977), Reiki, Energy Medicine, Palm Reading, intuition, reading energy patterns and many other highly specialized healing modalities.

With each new experience, my intuition and inner knowing increased to the point where I finally went beyond all of the teachings, doctrines, dogmas, tools and techniques I had experienced and learned. My intuition, guides and teachers showed me new approaches and new techniques — with many breakthroughs happening for my clients within a single session. Time, possibilities and even reality changed for me — and for the people I assisted. Many seemingly impossible things, including instantaneous energy clearings, life-changing healings and receiving important intuitive information for business clients, became possible, as well as every-day occurrences.

During the past 40 years, I have had the privilege of collaborating with and assisting the patients of other healers, therapists, chiropractors, holistic medical doctors, psychologists and even psychiatrists. To date, I have assisted many thousands of clients worldwide to break free of their limitations, balance their karma and become happier, healthier, more confident and more successful.

I have helped clients across the full spectrum of financial success: from the very poor to those who are extremely wealthy. Each person comes to me for a different reason. Many come for guidance, answers and solutions to challenges with their health, relationships, direction in life, children, finances, business, partnerships, sales, marketing and much more. Whatever a person is asking and seeking, there is usually guidance, an answer and a solution.

My clients report a variety of life-changing results: their healing process quickens and their spiritual growth accelerates. They gain greater access to their intuition and experience greater health, freedom, joy and happiness. They also report increased ease, grace, clarity, improved relationships, greater success and increased finances.

What surprised me the most was when I started to see entire businesses, companies and organizations, which were unique energy systems, with the same clarity as I had been seeing an individual's mental, physical, emotional and spiritual energy field. As a result, I am now able to intuitively look at and help a business in the same way, with the same speed and accuracy as I had been looking at an individual. This ability allows me to pinpoint where the disharmony and blockages were within the organization, to identify what was sabotaging the company and to know what is needed to clear them. It also shows me where the best and most lucrative business opportunities are. Entrepreneurs and organizations utilizing this information were able to quickly increase their effectiveness, efficiency and profitability.

Here is what it is like to have your intuitive awareness opened. This is an early spiritual experience I had while working with one of my teachers.

* * *

Observing Earth From The Spirit Realm

The curtains were drawn, allowing only the faintest light into the room. The acupuncture needles had been placed strategically to open my crown chakra (the energy center at the top of my head) and to my third eye (the area just above the bridge of my nose). This connected me to my Akashic records, a spiritual repository of all information from the beginning of time. My body was being massaged. Music designed to stimulate the process played softly in the background. My mind relaxed, drifted and let go of all thoughts.

All of a sudden, in my mind's eye, I clearly saw myself as a Divine Spiritual Being clothed in white flowing robes standing with a few other beings, dressed similarly. We were safely standing behind a single railing, looking down a large elongated opening in the floor — which was Earth's sky — closely observing the Earth's unfolding scenes below us.

From the peacefulness and safety of our reality, we were watching three-dimensional wars. Live. Compared to our tranquil, safe and enlightened state of being, these scenes appeared to be amazing, challenging and exciting, like a grand adventure.

As I watched, I felt a longing to join in. Little did I realize that actually being in the thick of a battle was completely different than observing it from a place of safety, emotional detachment and higher consciousness. From our vantage point — immortal and all knowing — we did not feel fear, suffering, pain, loss, doubt or confusion. To me, in my state of serene peacefulness, which bordered on boredom, everything on Earth seemed so alive, vibrant and exciting!

With this experience in the late 1970s and many more, I consciously started a new chapter of my spiritual journey.

***

Much like being at Disneyland, Six Flags over Texas and other adventure parks, the Earth adventure offers unique opportunities to lose ourselves in our experiences. Like all adventure parks, we can consciously or unconsciously choose where to go, what to participate in and how to react to, respond to and interpret our experiences.

If we prefer, we can also take the perspective of our Earth journey as entering into a giant schoolhouse with an infinite number of classes and lessons. Both of these models are very similar, as we come to Earth both to challenge ourselves and to learn.

As souls, we are committed to experiencing, learning, changing, growing, expanding and evolving. We are designed to be curious and to constantly experiment, test and challenge ourselves. The challenges we face and the wisdom we gain provide the fuel for our *Soul Growth*.

Like the immensity of the cosmos, opportunities for learning are infinite. Every soul is unique and learns in infinite ways. There are also an infinite number of lessons that a soul can choose to learn, an infinite number of places of learning, and an infinite number of universes and dimensions that a soul can choose from to learn these lessons.

Earth is only one of an infinite number of places of learning in the universe, all of which have been designed to offer and provide specific learning opportunities. People who choose to come to Earth are seeking to learn the specific lessons available here. If this were not true, there would be no reason to sign up for the Earth adventure park.

Prior to acquiring a ticket to any adventure park of learning, we are pure energy, pure consciousness and pure spirit, without a physical body. Between lifetimes, we go to a staging place that I call *Soul Space*.

It is a space from which we make decisions about what we want to learn and experience, and what adventure park we want to attend. While in Soul Space, we choose our major themes, lessons, nationality, race, parents, siblings, experiences, challenges, soul qualities and much more.

It's important to remember that we are the ones who choose, whether consciously or unconsciously, to experience everything that we experience here on Earth. There are no victims. Just the opposite! We are all immensely powerful master creators who are solely responsible for everything we consciously and unconsciously think, feel, attract, create and experience.

We have chosen to come to Earth to test ourselves, to learn our lessons and to become part of this great Earth experiment.

Some people go as far as to consider Earth to be more of a laboratory than an "adventure park" or "school house" where humans perform experiments, gather data, learn things and play with free will. These experiments either reveal new information and thus 'succeed;' or they 'fail' and thus give confirmation and support for the hypothesis; or, they go completely off the plans and make new maps that we learn to navigate by the trust, faith and seats of our pants.

Regardless of the model you feel most comfortable with and resonate with the most, Earth is definitely a unique place to choose to come to!

Acknowledgments

I wish to acknowledge and thank the many people who touched my life and made an everlasting impression upon my soul. Thank you for constantly challenging me, pushing me and supporting me to become a better person. Without your touching my life in many profound ways, I would not be the person I am today! Please know that if I included everyone who touched my life in a meaningful way, this list would be thousands of pages long. So please forgive me if your name is not listed here!

Two special people deeply touched my life; both transitioned during 2017. The first person is my beloved cousin, Stanley Gold who transitioned on November 22, 2017. Stan, who was 13 years older than me, was like an older brother to me.

We decided to terminate our relationship as family and to become friends instead. Stan and his wife, Bobbie, gave me the backup, support and home base I could rely on. I'm not sure I would be alive today, had it not been for their steadfast support and encouragement when I needed it the most. Thank you!

I had the honor and privilege of being totally present with my cousin, Stan, during his last three days on Earth, and was by his side touching his arm as he took his last breath. Thank you, Stan, for all of your love and support. Bless you and may your soul be at peace!

The second person is my college best friend and mentor, Hary Puente-Duany, who passed on May 20, 2017. I met Hary during my second year of college, and we became best friends and housemates. Hary changed my life, challenged me, rescued me from myself and helped me to find the good in myself. His family, who fled Cuba in the 1960s, was my first introduction to other cultures. Thank you, Hary. Bless you and may your soul be at peace.

Other people I wish to acknowledge are:

My family: my mother, Ruth, father, David, sister, Arlene, maternal grandmother, Yetta, maternal grandfather, Louis, Uncle Carl and Uncle Sam.

My mentors and supporters: Bert Bingaman, Dr. Julius Jackson, Jay Essinger, Jill Bounds, Elizabeth Francis, Weenie Witch and Mike Handcock. I also want to thank and acknowledge Hippocrates.

My personal friends: Gene Haller, Barbara Eves, Denny McArthur and family, Jasmail Singh and family, Olga Gouni, Paul Safe, Edith and Al Thomas, Carol Scott, Elspeth Kerr, Bobby Gill, Linda Schiller-Hanna, Dr. Janine Ambrose, Jackie Dunn, Peggy Cross, Suzanne Golden and Laurel Snyder.

My editors: Diane Eaton, Peggy Cross, Laurel Snyder and many others who helped to nurture and polish this book. A special thank you to the wonderful creative artist, Ciara, who designed the book cover.

The sacred lands of Sedona, Machu Picchu, The Wailing Wall, Delphi, The Great Pyramids, The Greek Asclepius (temples and healing centers), Uluru, Nepal, New Zealand and all other sacred lands.

I honor a number of spiritual groups, including The Councils and Tribunals of Light, the White Brotherhood, the Emerald Brotherhood, the Sisterhoods of Light, the Karmic Board, and the Lords and Ladies of Light.

I also honor *All My Relations,* including the Extra Terrestrials, Inter-Dimensionals, Inter-Galactic Beings, the Angels, Arch-Angels, Devas, Inner Earth Beings and all the Kingdoms; The

Elements Earth, Air, Fire, Water, Wood, Metal and Ether; The Native American spirits; The Two Legged, the Four Legged, the Plant People (especially the Kawa Kawa plant), the Tree People, the Stone People, the Water People, the Air People, the Fire People, the Winged Ones, the Finned Ones and the Creepy Crawlies.

I invite, welcome, thank, honor and bless *All My Relations* who come in a good and sacred way!

Introduction

Have you ever felt lost, lonely, isolated, frustrated, overwhelmed or confused? Have you ever asked yourself any of the following questions?

Who am I?

What am I doing here?

What is my soul purpose for being here?

Have you ever felt like Earth was not your real home and that somehow you really didn't fit in or belong here? Have you wondered where you are really from? Do you want a better understanding of how to thrive beyond just surviving on the Earth plane?

This book offers answers to many of your questions and provides insights into new ways of looking at and understanding your Earth adventure.

As you read, allow yourself to relax, sense, feel and savor the information. This book is designed to help activate and awaken you to who you truly are. It is also designed to help you remember the real reasons why you came to Earth and the lessons you have chosen to learn. In fact, somewhere deep inside, you already unconsciously know everything I'm going to share. This book is designed to rekindle your inner knowing and to bring this information to the level of conscious awareness.

This book will also give you the understanding that will allow you to better navigate the challenges you will most likely encounter during your lifetime here on Earth.

Consider this:

Before starting any vacation, holiday or journey, most of us have a number of questions. We want to know our destination, how long we will be gone, what mode of transportation we will use to get there, where we will stay, what to take with us, how much it will cost and what activities we will participate in. We will also want to know the health and safety conditions of our destination, as well as what clothes and special equipment to take with us. People are rarely courageous enough to randomly pick a holiday destination, without having specific reasons for going, knowing what to expect when they arrive or having a detailed plan. Before they book a trip, most people do their research and surf the internet, talk to travel agents, read brochures and review maps.

Before we are born on this planet, we go through a process of choosing that is very similar to the process of planning the trip described above. It is a journey that all of us have chosen to take, although most of us have forgotten the very reasons why we booked this *Earth Adventure*. By design, we have been programmed to forget our Inner Knowing and our Divinity.

We've also forgotten that we *specifically requested* the challenges we now face. These challenges enable us to test our strength, courage, abilities and convictions. The blocking of these memories is all part of the *Divine Plan* and is for our highest good. If we were aware of the tests and trials we signed up for, it would change the way we approach them. So we masterfully keep ourselves in the dark. How could we truly test ourselves if we already had the answer sheets in hand?

The information in this book is designed to assist you in navigating your journey and tapping into your forgotten inner knowing. Having a road map and remembering the big picture will help you better understand yourself, your thoughts, your feelings and your emotions. It also helps you to better understand your challenges, and the reasons you are going through your many tests and trials. This clarity can help you to discover the fastest, easiest, most gentle and most compassionate way through your challenges.

Once you start to reconnect with your inner knowing, intuition and wisdom, you have the opportunity to increase your *Soul Frequency* and *Soul Vibration*. This, in turn, can greatly accelerate your *Soul Growth* and help you attract more ease, grace, love, joy, happiness and success into your life.

***

A long time ago, I wrote these words:

> **The greatest gift you can ever give someone else is something that you always wanted, craved and never received.**

Several advanced beings and people who channel information have revealed to me that my life mission and purpose on this Earth plane is to "teach the teachers and heal the healers." Everything I write and teach is designed to guide and support you on your personal journey to Self, oneness, freedom, healing and unity with Source.

In this book, I share my personal journey with you, along with many of the answers that I've spent my life searching for. This is my truth, as best I know it at this point in my journey.

I hope that it is a gift to you.

Many Blessings, Namaste, All My Relations, Om Shanti
Your Soul Friend and Fellow Earth Traveler,
Michael Bradford

Table of Contents

When You Are Ready

When you are ready
Your life will begin to change
And the past, with all its hurts, pains
And disappointments will gently melt away.

When you are ready
Your confusion, resistance, fears and doubts will dissipate
And your desire for freedom will grow
Beckoning you to fully embrace the real you.

When you are ready
Your mask, your survival kit, will no longer be needed
And the true you, the authentic you,
Will gingerly peek out seeking the light of life.

When you are ready
Your pride, looking good and being right will no longer matter
For your desire for truth, connection and spirit
Will awaken and fill you.

And when you are ready
Your vision will clear and you will know, beyond the shadow of
      a doubt
The gift that you already are.
It is time, beloved being of light, to ignite and shine bright!

Chapter 1
Arriving on Earth

Why Did We Choose Earth?

Earth is one of the most beautiful, unique, special planets, adventure parks and places of learning in the entire universe — and one of the most challenging. Compared to the expanse of learning opportunities in the universe, some people consider Earth to be like kindergarten. The truth is that Earth is a place where very advanced beings, even masters, come to test themselves to see if they can keep their balance here and remain true to themselves. Even advanced souls frequently get distracted and seduced by the Earth's tests, trials and temptations. When this happens, souls get caught up on the *Wheel of Karma.*

The Earth is such an amazing adventure park and place of learning that an extremely long line of souls is waiting to incarnate and test themselves here. Because we forget this, many people do not appreciate how special being here is and what a great opportunity we have on Earth.

Some who graduated the Earth plane have volunteered to come back as healers, teachers and guides to help the people and the Earth with their transition/evolution into higher realms of consciousness. These people are called *Bodhisattvas.*

What Makes Earth So Challenging?

Throughout much of the universe, unity, peace and harmony exist. Beings are immortal, invincible and all knowing. In most dimensions of the universe, all you have to do is imagine something and it is instantly manifested with little or no effort. On the Earth plane, however, we live within the illusions of time, separation, duality, mortality, pain, suffering, lack, vulnerability, polarity and density.

The duality and polarities within our collective illusion create an extremely challenging environment. They include male/female, right/wrong, good/bad, head/heart, masculine/feminine, logic/intuition, material/spiritual, love/hate, pleasure/pain and abundance/poverty. In addition to polarities, there are the powerful temptations of mortality, money, power, greed, sex and religion that set the stage for a very wide range of tests and trials.

Just so we don't get bored, we have the additional challenge of manifesting what we want and desire on the Earth plane. On many other planets and in other dimensions, all one has to do is to think of something and it instantaneously manifests. However, because Earth exists in third dimensional reality, which has a much lower frequency and vibration than the dimensions most of us originate from, the manifestation process here is much slower and takes much more focus, concentration, time and effort. The denser energy on Earth changes the process of manifestation from an instantaneous one to a process that takes much greater intention, time, energy, effort and focus. These factors often create enormous stress, frustration and anxiety in many people.

There are many more challenges, too.

Before We Come to Earth

With the assistance of our team of guides, teachers and advisors, our soul meets to review our *Cosmic Report Card*, the sum total of all of our learning experiences from the beginning of time. This meeting is to determine which adventure park and learning lessons are most appropriate for the next stage of our soul's growth. Once we've selected the Earth plane as our best path of learning, we choose and plan what we will focus on to learn and experience. Our spiritual coaches are much like the guidance counselors we had in high school, however they are infinitely wiser. Usually they are not the same ones who will remain with us and guide us during our time on Earth, although they can be. I intuitively see souls meet with several very wise advisors who assist them as they evaluate their soul's progress and choose this lifetime's themes.

If we were left to our own naive decision-making process, without the wisdom of our advisors, we would most likely choose challenges that are totally appropriate for an invincible, immortal, all knowing, spiritual being, however they would be totally unrealistic, impractical and inappropriate for anyone incarnating into the density and challenges of the Earth. In fact, this is one of the reasons guides and teachers — especially those who have never physically incarnated onto Earth and experienced Earth lifetimes — have so much difficulty in understanding why *Earthlings* have such a challenging time and do not instantly "get it" when their guides offer help and suggestions. From the guides' perspective, everything appears so easy! But they don't have a clue what it is really like, until they are born into the dense, heavy, polarity energy of Earth and have to deal with Earthly conditions, such as mortality, fear, loss, pain, suffering, having to work, things taking a long time to manifest and so on.

Decisions We Make Prior to Arriving on Earth

When we meet with our spiritual advisors prior to birth on Earth, they help us select the major themes and primary life lessons we'll focus on learning at this stage of our development. We'll choose a great variety of things, including the country where we will be born, our parents, siblings, social status, race, culture, health, financial status, gender, sexual orientation, physical appearance, major life learning lessons and much more. We also choose whether we will experience being loved, nurtured and supported — or whether we'll be unloved, unsupported, beaten, abused, and have our self-image and self-esteem crushed.

It is important to note we are never allowed to take on more than we can handle. Along with our challenges and soul lessons, we are also given resources and strengths to support us as we learn to break free of our limitations. It is up to us to discover, develop and use these resources. Some of us will completely break free of our dysfunctional and destructive patterns. Others will only partially break free and will still have residue to clear at the end of this lifetime. We all have the opportunity to come back again in our next lifetime in order to clear any unresolved issues and unfinished business.

If there is not enough mental, physical, emotional or spiritual energy to totally break free, a person may keep slipping back into their old patterns and temptations over and over again until, finally, they accumulate sufficient energy, knowledge, strength and wisdom to totally break free of their limitations.

As we descend from higher spiritual levels into the dense third-dimensional Earth plane, we forget who we truly are. Although we consciously choose all of our Earth challenges and lessons, we forget that we chose them. We also inevitably forget that we are wise, all knowing, invincible and immortal spiritual beings.

By the way, the most advanced souls choose the greatest challenges.

The Veil

When our soul leaves the spirit realm and descends into the density of the Earth plane, we disconnect from and leave behind our spiritual support system and our inner knowing as immortal spiritual beings. As spirit, everything is very clear, easy and simple — we know that we are all powerful and all knowing, and we can easily see the truth of who we are. We exist in total awareness and total oneness. But when we reach the Earth plane, this is no longer the case. This is called *The Veil* and when it closes, like a curtain closing, we become disconnected from our full spiritual inner power, inner knowing and divine perspective.

As we descend into the world of duality and the heavy, dense energy of the Earth plane, some of us panic. This is especially true for those souls just coming to Earth for the first time or who have only been on Earth a few times. These people can feel severely disoriented and it may take them a number of lifetimes to finally fully adjust, relax and feel comfortable with the radical change of descending into the dense Earth vibration.

Making the transition to the Earth plane can be extremely shocking; our spiritual power, spiritual connection, spiritual knowing, spiritual family and everything else that we have cherished and held sacred are left behind. When this happens, we may feel alone, lost, lonely, isolated, depressed, hopeless, abandoned and even betrayed.

Leaving our spiritual home and descending into the density of the Earth plane energies is a human being's first major challenge.

Conception and Beyond

When a human egg is conceived, there is a bio-energetic imprint created by the interaction of the sperm and the egg. A number of radically different energies can greatly affect the energy of the fetus during conception. As the union occurs, several energies combine, including the energy of the father, the energy of the mother, the energy of the land, the energy of their interaction and those of the surroundings where the union occurred. All of these energies affect and imprint upon the conceived child as it is launched onto the Earth plane.

A number of radically different energies can greatly affect the energy of a fetus at the instant of conception. For example, the father's and the mother's energies convey their level of spiritual development, their thoughts, attitudes, beliefs and the clarity of their unique energy fields. The fetus' surroundings convey information about whether the environment was calm, peaceful and a sacred place or if the energy was negative, scrambled and traumatic, such as being in a war zone. Other factors are also carried through, such as whether or not the acts of penetration, impregnation and fertilization were ones of affection, consent, love and respect, or if they were acts of violence without consent.

If the conception experience involved aggression, violence, abuse or trauma, then the conceived child may absorb these energies, along with the mother's feelings of anger, fear, resentment, shame, duty, brutality, violence, rape and disgust. These qualities can affect and sabotage the child, on a conscious and unconscious level, for his entire life, unless he receives help.

On the other hand, if conception happened in an atmosphere of love, happiness, affection and welcoming, this stage of development will be clear, calm and peaceful. Hence, this will not present any added challenges to the conceived child.

Some souls choose to come into the Earth plane embodying a lot of negative energy, while others choose to come in with a lot of positive energy. Either way, a unique energy imprint is created, which allows the soul to either embrace or overcome these energies, and learn very different lessons. From the perspective of the soul and the higher realms of consciousness, there is no good or bad, no right or wrong. It is all just learning!

The soul can enter a conceived child as early as the moment of conception, but doesn't have to. My intuition tells me that they do so about 70% of the time, otherwise they come in later in the pregnancy. When the soul does arrive into the physical body, a spark, a presence and an energy shift occur.

Some intuitives have observed newborn babies struggling to fully incarnate and to settle into their physical bodies. This may be because many souls have spirit bodies that are much larger than their human physical body and they need energy adjustments (energetic healing) to help them relax more fully, settle in and incarnate. There can be additional challenges in the process, too, if a soul is anxious, impatient, scared or has been traumatized.

To assist with this process, I use my intuitive energy tracking abilities to pinpoint exactly what the challenge is and what energy healing is needed to help.

* * *

Jane, an attractive Italian woman in her late 40s, was uncomfortable in her body and felt challenged by intimate relationships. As I scanned her energy field, I could see that the energy surrounding her conception was one of force and aggression. The energy had permeated and contaminated her body and energy field, and was negatively affecting her relationships. In her session, I assisted her in clearing the fear, pain and discordant energy, and I helped her reclaim her own energy and freedom.

* * *

In the mid-1980s, I created a meditation to help a friend's daughter who was having challenges during her pregnancy. The unborn child in her womb was very active and was creating substantial back pain for her.

The expectant mother discovered that whenever she played the meditation, the baby inside her would relax, calm down and stop kicking. So she played it frequently before the child was born and she later played it in the delivery room. In fact, she even played it to help calm down her newborn daughter after delivery and as the child was growing up.

Years later, a teenage girl I had never met came up to me at a meeting I was attending and said, "I'd know your voice anywhere! You are the one who made the meditation for me many years ago!" She thanked me and told me how much it had helped her to relax and cope with life!

* * *

While in a business meeting in Asia, Bill, a senior partner in an investment firm, mentioned he was both excited and concerned because his wife, Ann, was pregnant again. Ann had miscarried twice already and he and his wife were very concerned that she might not be able to carry the new pregnancy to full term.

Immediately, I intuitively sensed that, under the current energetic conditions, the unborn child would also be miscarried. Sharing my concerns with Bill, I highly recommended that both he and his wife have a joint healing session with me. Normally I only see people individually, however I was intuitively guided to see them together.

In their healing session, Bill and Ann both shared with me that they had been sexually abused as children. Because of their painful childhood abuse, they were adamant that they did not want to bring any child into this world unless they could guarantee the child's safety.

During their session, they shared the painful and humiliating details of their abuse. As they talked, they cried, releasing much of their internalized suppressed pain and suffering. This emotional release cleared a lot of the trapped discordant energy that was affecting their mindset and energetically blocking their ability to carry a child full term.

Once the energy was released, I helped them realize that they could only do their best and that there are never any guarantees in life. I emphasized that the child had its own destiny to fulfill and no matter what they wanted, the child had to be free to experience life fully.

This new perspective regarding their level of responsibility as a parent released a lot of old, deep-seated anger, hurt, fear, guilt, shame and blame. As both of them energetically discharged and cleared, I could sense their energy fields shifting and aligning to a higher frequency.

I am happy to report that, after their single one-hour session, Ann and Bill gave birth to a lovely healthy child. After the child was born, they called me to thank me for the session. They said that without it, they doubted if they would be holding a healthy child in their arms!

In Bill and Ann's case, the unresolved blocked emotional energy, and the conscious and unconscious fears of both parents, sabotaged and blocked any child from staying full term, and being born healthy. With other clients, I experienced how similar unresolved fears, anxieties and traumas have sabotaged the conception process, the pregnancy and the birthing process.

I intuitively estimate that a full 90% of all challenges with getting pregnant, from both the male and female perspective, and maintaining the pregnancy full term, are caused by a combination of mental, physical, emotional, spiritual and energetic blockages.

Although these may appear to be medical issues and the medical establishment will usually find reasons and remedies for these issues, I find the deepest root cause of almost all health, healing and life challenges — including allergies, diabetes, thyroid problems, hepatitis C and even cancer — to be caused by energetic blockages.

Time in the Womb

Once a human egg is conceived, it attaches itself to the lining of the mother's womb. While attached, the unborn child has consciousness, however it cannot differentiate between itself and its mother; the unborn child believes that it and the mother are one. During this time, the fetus is completely dependent upon its mother for protection and sustenance. As there is a constant flow of nutrients and energy back and forth between the fetus and the mother, the fetus naturally shares and absorbs the positive or negative energies and emotions of the mother.

There are number of factors that affect the mental, physical, emotional and spiritual health of a developing child. They include the mental, physical, emotional and spiritual state and energies of the mother and the father, the availability of adequate nutritious food and pure water, the environment, the weather and more.

If there is peace and harmony between the parents and in the environment, the embryo can develop without absorbing any trauma. However if the parents fight frequently or if the environment is otherwise filled with conflict, there is a good chance that the child will absorb these disharmonious energies and be traumatized.

When the mother is healthy, happy and energetically balanced and when there is peace, harmony, good nutrition and plenty of resources in the environment, it can be a joyful and relaxing time for the fetus to develop. If the mother is sick or experiencing violence, abuse, fear, disharmony, anger, trauma, fighting, war in the region, famine or grief, the discordant energy can negatively impact the developing fetus.

Because there are no energetic boundaries between a unborn child and its mother, the emerging embryo and fetus, in an attempt to protect and stabilize the mother, may attempt to absorb the discordant negative energy from the mother and will give the mother its positive energy. Since the main goal of the unborn child is to stay alive, it will automatically give up its own positive energy to ensure the mother's survival.

This experience in the womb can set up a lifelong imprinted pattern called a *Prenatal Healer*. Here the unborn child develops, believing that its main purpose in life — its ego and personality identity — is of someone who takes care of and fixes others. When this happens, for the rest of this child's life, in order to feel wanted, loved, worthy and safe, the child may have an overriding need to protect, rescue, fix and heal their parents, twin, siblings, partners, children and others. Here the energetic, emotional, imprinted unconscious belief is: *"I have to save you — control you, fix you, keep the peace, and make sure you are safe and happy. Only by saving you first, can I ever hope to save myself and feel safe."*

Far from being a highly spiritual experience, this behavior entraps the unborn child into a life of co-dependency, keeping quiet, playing small, being invisible, attracting dysfunctional people, being a rescuer, staying longer in abusive relationships than is healthy and living a life of deprivation among other things.

The Prenatal Healer is only one of the many dysfunctional, self-sabotaging scripts that may start while the unborn child is developing. Using various healing modalities and especially the intuitive energy tracking and clearing methods I have developed, these patterns can be identified and healed.

* * *

Stephen was a Greek man in his late 60s who was often nervous and insecure. Even though he was very intelligent, talented and successful, he didn't feel safe around people or trust life. In session with Stephen, I intuitively tracked his energy and discovered that his father never wanted children.

Stephen told me that when his father found out that his new wife was pregnant with Stephen, his father punched his wife in the stomach and threw her down a flight of stairs. My inner sight also saw that Stephen was originally a twin, and that his twin was a sister. However when Stephen's father punched his mother, his twin sister was killed. No one had ever known about it.

With this new awareness, Stephen allowed himself to grieve for three months after the session. As he integrated the new information, he was able to better understand why he had always felt so unsafe and did not trust life. He is now making good progress.

* * *

Paula was a divorced Costa Rican woman in her early 50s with a 17-year-old son, Richard. He was the center of her life. In session, I immediately sensed something was very wrong with their connection; in fact, they were extremely energetically enmeshed. As I monitored their energies, I saw something I had never seen before or since. Paula and her son had a single energy field. There was no separation. There was no individuation. In an attempt to have someone to love and connect with, Paula had actually merged her energy with her son's to the point where they were extensions of each other. Although this occasionally happens with a fetus, I had never seen it in a young child, teenager or adult. It was neither healthy nor appropriate. I talked with them explaining what I was seeing and then helped them to gain more of a sense of their own true selves and to let go of their entanglements. Being energetically enmeshed with another person is co-dependent and dysfunctional, even among partners or twins.

* * *

Cynthia, an Asian woman in her late 50s, came to see me with Carol, her 19-year-old daughter who was living with her. Cynthia complained that Carol was listless and depressed, and was not helping around the house or even communicating. When I looked at their energy fields, I was surprised to see that they both shared the same energy field. When I talked to Cynthia about it, she said that Carol had developed diabetes when she was about 9 years old, the age when Cynthia and her husband had separated. Cynthia had to stay around day and night to give her daughter the shots she required. She was terrified that if she was not vigilant, her daughter would die.

In session, Cynthia expressed that she was from a culture where women were suppose to remain subservient to men and take care of the family. After Cynthia's divorce, rather than going out and forming a healthy adult dating relationship, she stayed to herself and clung onto her daughter. All of these factors contributed to the inappropriate bonding (dysfunctional energy enmeshment) between them. I explained to Cynthia and Carol that their connection was too close and was enmeshed, and therefore was stifling both of them. This is known as classic co-dependency. As we talked, I could see their energy fields start to separate and individuate. This was the first step in their healing process, as well as their quest for independence and freedom.

Birth on Earth

Many psychologists, therapists and healers consider the human birth experience to be one of the major events affecting our lives. Likewise, studies have found that the way we experienced the timing of our birth is often the way we interact with life for the rest of our lives. When a child is born early, on time or late, it can affect his personality and patterns in life.

I wholeheartedly believe that the consciousness and the soul purpose of the fetus help to determine its birthing experience. In turn, the birthing experience has an affect on the consciousness and life path of the child after she is born. Both are true.

Souls who are born early compared to their expected birth date tend to be excited and comfortable about arriving on Earth. They want to get on with things. Just as they've arrived early on Earth, they also tend to arrive early for appointments, they tend to finish projects early and they are otherwise early with most things in life. As children, they are typically excited about life and living; they are impatient, they want to complete things quickly, they are proactive and they often become leaders.

When a soul is born right on schedule, it can indicate that she is relaxed, comfortable and in harmony with the natural flow of life. She will tend to go with the flow, to arrive on time for events and be more relaxed, at peace and in balance with her surroundings and interactions.

Souls that are late for arrival may tend to be resistant, scared and possibly stubborn. They are more likely to procrastinate and often arrive late for appointments, meetings and other events during their entire life. Their late birth arrival can indicate a resistance or fear of being born on Earth, or difficulty staying fully present in their body and participating fully in life. Some of these beings may be so resistant to life that medical procedures have to be employed to induce birth.

* * *

When I was describing these three very different birthing patterns at a presentation in Asia, a woman in her late 40s jumped up and shouted, "Thank you. That explains a lot. I have three teenagers at home — one of each of the birth scenarios and corresponding personality types you have just described!"

* * *

A woman who described her lifelong "fight" with time asked me whether this "programming" could be reset and changed. I told her that I believe we can change and heal just about anything and everything, as long as we are committed to learning, changing and evolving.

Birth to Age Seven

The time period from birth to age seven is critical in the development of a child into a healthy responsible adult. During that time, children do not have strong boundaries and are mentally, physically, emotionally, spiritually and energetically open, receptive, vulnerable and impressionable. They are like soft clay that can be easily molded. Young children are like sponges, absorbing all the information and energy around them. The challenge is that young children do not yet have a strong identity, energetic boundaries, knowledge, filters, reference points or the experience to discern whether the information they are learning and the energies they are absorbing are true and helpful, or false and harmful to them. They have not yet achieved the maturity of discernment to know the difference between healthy and dysfunctional behavior.

This developmental period is similar to building the foundation of a house. If the foundation is not well built and does not have structural integrity, no matter what you build on top of it, it will never achieve the potential it could have had if the foundation had been stable, solid and strong. That is why it is so critical to teach children strong positive values and ethics at a young age. Children need positive role models.

Children learn by listening, watching, sensing, feeling and interacting with their parents, siblings, extended family, neighbors, TV, environment, religious organizations, schools and other children. It is very important for young children to be taught love, respect, kindness, honesty, integrity, values, ethics, communication, support, nurturing and safety, and to eat healthy foods. They also need to learn healthy boundaries and interaction skills.

It is the responsibility of parents, family members, society, organizations, religions and schools to be positive role models, and to teach children healthy values and interaction skills. If positive values are not taught to young people, they will become more susceptible to being molded by the negative behavior, disrespect and the violence so prevalent in today's TV programs, video games and movies. When a child has a solid positive foundation, the child has a much greater chance of learning to think positively, act and interact in positive ways, and become independent.

Young children need our guidance, direction and support. They also need to learn limits, boundaries and respect for creating and interacting with the Earth, including the land, animals, plants and people. This respect must be instilled at an early age or there is a risk of a child growing up believing that it is acceptable to lie, cheat, steal, harm or even kill others.

One of the challenges is to teach children respect and values without destroying their curiosity, spontaneity and creativity. Channeling a child's curiosity, energy and passion into positive programs and projects takes skill and maturity on the part of parents, family members, guardians and teachers.

If a child's parents, teachers and role models did not receive this positive support as they were growing up, it makes it very challenging for them to know how to do this effectively for a child. This is part of the challenge and the main reason why dysfunctional behavior is passed down for generations.

When children of different races, colors, socio-economic backgrounds and countries are growing up, these children play together peacefully (or at least normally) and seldom experience the same fears, anxiety, struggles, aggression, prejudices or class discrimination that happens among many adults. Judgment, prejudice, separation and inequality, whether towards a person, group or a nation, are learned behaviors.

Almost all young children have a natural connection to spirits, angels and other "invisible friends" until they are teased, criticized and told that what they are experiencing is not real. When this happens, most children will shut the door to this connection in an attempt to fit in, be accepted and to appear normal. This teasing — and the desire to feel safe, fit in and appear normal — may cause the child, young adult or even adult to block their intuition, psychic sight and spiritual connections.

Skilled energy healing and coaching can help to clear the traumas of early childhood and can help build a new, healthy emotional and psychological foundation, even for the adults that they've grown to become.

My healing and coaching work focuses on helping my clients to identify these early blockages, clear them and positively re-parent their inner child. When a client is committed, this healing and rebuilding process can be achieved fairly quickly.

* * *

When I was 17 years old, I worked as a counselor at a summer camp where there were many underprivileged children from broken homes. One young African American boy, about 9 years old, was constantly in trouble for creating problems. He was being disruptive, fighting, complaining, resisting and was always last on hikes.

One day, I took time out to talk with him. I asked him about his life and what he wanted to be when he grew up. Without any hesitation, he said, "I want to be a Marine!" From that moment on, I coached him on how I believed Marines thought, acted and became leaders.

After our talk, he totally changed. From that day on, he became the leader of the group. He even started carrying another boy's backpack in addition to his own; until then, he had been complaining about having to carry his own. His attitude changed completely; he began helping to solve problems instead of creating them.

There is no doubt in my mind that had this child not developed some positive role models, he could easily have fallen into a life of addictions and/or crime. I wonder where this precious child is now and what he has achieved in his life. I also wonder if and how our interaction impacted his life long term?

Interacting with Other People's Energy

Imagine a glass of water that is filled to the brim and unable to hold any more. If you dropped something into the glass, its physical volume would displace the exact same volume of water in the glass and cause it to overflow. It's basic physics: two physical objects cannot occupy the same space at the same time.

The same principle applies on an bioenergetic level when we take on other people's energies, or when we consciously or unconsciously give away our own energy to help others. For example, imagine that we have 100% of our energy available to us. When we give our energy away to others, our energy levels may become lessened, contaminated or even depleted. When we take on the pain and suffering of others, we may give them our positive energy and absorb their painful negative energy. Taking on other people's pain and suffering does not help them to learn their lessons and this definitely does not help us. All of these actions will compromise, deplete and displace our own positive life-force energy, filling us with the other person's negative energy.

I have found that the single most telling indicator of a person's health, happiness, wellbeing, prosperity and success is whether or not they are fully energetically present in their physical body. Only a few of my clients have been more than 30% energetically present in their physical body at the time they came to me. Most were only between 5% and 20% present.

So far, after assisting many thousands of clients, I have only tracked the energy of five people who were more than 30% energetically present in their physical body. Yet, when I saw one of them years later, I noticed that he had dropped back to under 30%. And he was not happy.

To be truly happy, healthy and successful, we must be authentic and be energetically present in our bodies!

Some of the reasons people are not fully present in their bodies include: failure to fully incarnate, unresolved trauma at conception, trauma in the womb, negative programming, loss, shock, trauma, accidents, fear, belief in self-sacrifice, past-life trauma, karma, death of a loved one or pet, vows, promises or commitments to others. There may also be energetic contamination, enmeshment and negative energy attachments. These unresolved challenges can originate in this lifetime, or be carried forward from past lifetimes on Earth or even from other dimensions.

It's important to remember that all of these challenges can be identified, healed and cleared. Each one of us can transform what holds us back and become more energetically present. Sally's story, described below, explains the depths to which this can affect us.

* * *

As the room was filling for my introductory evening talk, my attention was drawn to a woman who had just entered the room. Her energy was very heavy and scrambled, plus she did not seem to take very good care of herself. For some reason, I had an immediate negative reaction to her energy. I thought, "Who let this woman in?" I confess to being judgmental in that moment, but it set up one of the most powerful learning lessons of my life! To my amazement she sat down in the front row, directly in front of me.

At the end of my two-hour presentation and demonstration, this woman raised her hand to ask a question. When I asked how I could serve her, she dropped her head and, looking down at the floor, said in a very shaky, stuttering, childlike voice, "Michael, I am 58 years old. I have never worked. I have been in and out of mental institutions all of my life. I am on medications and under a doctor's care. Is there any hope for a person like me?"

Her name was Sally. To read her energy, I had to open my heart and my energy field to her, and when I did I almost burst into tears. I was shocked by what I saw.

I said to her, "There is absolutely nothing wrong with you. But your mother was crazy, wasn't she?" Sally nodded her head and said, "Yes," while still looking at the floor. I told her, "All you ever wanted was to feel safe and to have a happy childhood, but you never got it, did you?" She shook her head from side to side and said "No, No" and continued to look down at the floor.

Over the next few minutes I explained to Sally that the mental illness she had been diagnosed with was not energetically hers. It was her mother's energy that the doctors were picking up on. I told her that, as a fetus and a young child, in an attempt to stabilize her mother's erratic and insane energy, she had taken on and absorbed much of her mother's negative energy into her own body. At the same time, she had given her mother over 90% of her own positive life force energy. This left Sally with her mother's scrambled energy in her body and very little of her own positive energy. In fact, Sally probably had only about 2% of her own energy in her body when she walked into the room that evening.

Sally asked me how she might attend my workshop that weekend, since she didn't have the money to pay for it. Stunned and impressed by her heartfelt desire and commitment, I told her not to worry about the money. I told her that if she were really committed to learning, changing and growing, I would assist her in every way I could. I also made it perfectly clear to her that it was her responsibility to learn to support herself.

Sally attended the weekend workshop, stayed focused and worked harder than most of the other attendees. She had many breakthroughs, releasing her mother's energy and reclaiming her own energy. As a result, her energy cleared and she transformed into a new person. What she achieved in one weekend was amazing and life-changing for her!

A few weeks after the workshop, I received a phone call from the workshop organizer, telling me that Sally was losing weight, was coming off her medication, had just been hired by Pizza Hut and was finally enjoying life. This was her very first job and she was flying! Although we lost touch after the workshop, Sally continues to be one of my greatest teachers, showing me and everyone else, what is possible! Hers is one of the most heartbreaking and heart-warming cases I've ever experienced, and it taught me how a sensitive child can give up her entire life to stabilize a parent.

Please note that my reaction to Sally when she entered the room was a reaction to her mother's scrambled discordant energy, which was in her energy field. It was not a reaction to the essence of Sally's soul, which was pure. This is very telling: we sometimes react to people — or they may react to us — because of what we read from them energetically.

The Power of Early Childhood Decisions

Children have very little understanding and experience when it comes to making healthy decisions. Unfortunately, this is also true for many adults since few adults have done their own deep inner healing work.

As children grow up, they learn by observing and interacting with many others: their parents, other children, extended family, school, community and other adults they might model after. They are also greatly influenced by religious teachings, television, movies and video games. If a child is exposed to and interacts with healthy and functional role models, the child has a chance of learning healthy ways of thinking, communicating and interacting. Unfortunately there are very few, if any, totally functional healthy families. To some degree, most families are dysfunctional and codependent, and as a result they do not demonstrate healthy interaction skills.

Few children are raised in an environment that is always calm, relaxed and positive, where they can grow up safe, trusting and inquisitive. Many children have been raised in environments where at least one adult was volatile and the atmosphere included sarcasm, anger, aggression, abuse, yelling, intimidation and lashing out. On the other extreme, one adult may have been very quiet, withdrawn, depressed and shut down. Experiencing this even one time, especially if it involved mental, physical, emotional, spiritual or sexual abuse, can negatively affect a child for his entire life.

When a child experiences a shock, trauma, loss, accident or other painful event, he usually reacts. His mind will usually try to make meaning out of the pain and chaos, so he can understand it, avoid it and survive. This is done instantaneously, as a knee-jerk reaction to the event.

Unfortunately, these strategies for surviving are often limiting and incorrect. They are created in an instant, without any reflection or any understanding of the situation, or the options available. From that point forward, those erroneous decisions will limit the possibility for the child to develop and interact with life in a healthy manner.

In contrast to this, a healthy mature fully functional adult faced with making a major decision that will affect her for her entire life will take her time, do some research, talk to experts, search the Internet, consult with experienced coaches and mentors, and will not make a final decision until she feels comfortable she has reached the best decision possible.

As a result of the imperfect and possibly even self-destructive decisions made as a child, adults have to go back and re-evaluate both their conscious and subconscious limiting decisions and beliefs that they've made about life and living. My intuition tells me that only about 20% of the decisions children made in order to emotionally and sometimes physically survive a situation were appropriate and healthy ones. The remaining 80% of decisions end up sabotaging and limiting an adult's ability to be happy and healthy, to have good relationships and to experience the good things in life, such as health, joy, happiness, peace, love, success and abundance.

When I intuitively scan a person's energy field, I am able to identify these limiting decisions and patterns, and to help my client to release the old programs. Once released, I assist my client to create new more functional life-affirming decisions. When the decisions made as a child are identified and reviewed with the eyes of an adult, and especially with the help of an experienced intuitive healer, a client can quickly and easily identify and integrate healthier, more appropriate options and strategies for creating a happy, healthy and prosperous life.

* * *

Peggy was an Australian woman in her late 30s who had suffered from hypertension and anxiety since childhood. All of her life she had studied hard, wanted to understand everything and felt driven to know all of the answers. She was very afraid that she would miss something. No matter how much she studied and learned, she had to study more and learn more. She never felt like she understood or learned enough.

When I looked at her energy field, I saw that she had been a twin in the womb and her twin brother's embryo had died at about three months in utero. His spirit body had actually survived and energetically entered Peggy's energy field. Because of this, there were a couple of factors affecting Peggy. The first challenge was that her brother, by being in her energy field, was limiting her ability to access her authentic feminine energy, feelings and emotions. He was also preventing her from fully embracing her own life mission and purpose. Making matters even more challenging was the fact that it was her brother's energy — not hers — that was so afraid and thus frantically seeking answers. The presence of her brother's energy was scrambling Peggy's energy field, causing her to be afraid and unsure.

When I shared these insights with Peggy, her eyes filled with tears, her face flushed and her emotional body began releasing her lifelong trauma. When I asked Peggy if she could feel herself grieving, she said she could not feel anything. She could not feel it because she was not connected to her own authentic feelings and emotions.

As the entire process only took a few minutes, it was then up to Peggy to decide whether she would make the commitment to reconnect with her authentic self. Each of us is always at choice as to whether to take positive action to heal ourselves or continue to remain disconnected. Peggy never contacted me after our initial meeting. I can only hope and trust that she someday makes the commitment to reconnect with her authentic self.

Note: There was another healer present in the room when I worked with Peggy, and she was amazed at the emotional release Peggy was going through. Even though Peggy was going through these emotions and other people could easily see her reactions — Peggy felt nothing.

* * *

Caroline was in her late 30s and living in California when she came for a session with me. From the age of five, she had suffered from hypertension. As her family was wealthy, they took her to the best medical professionals in the world. Unfortunately, no one was able to help her. As I tuned into her energy field, I sensed that something had happened between her and her father, which triggered her hypertension. Intuitively, I saw her father bathing her as a child and the towel rubbing up against her genital area.

This innocent movement of the towel had confused her and triggered an energetic and emotional reaction in her that she did not understand. Although her father had not done anything inappropriate, the movement of the towel triggered the reaction, causing Caroline to react and shut down. As I shared this information with Caroline and energetically cleared the trauma from her body, she broke down and cried as her body relaxed for the first time in many years. The entire session lasted one hour.

Without being able to intuitively see energies and access other dimensions, it is much more challenging to understand what is really happening beneath the surface of our thoughts, feelings, emotions, experiences and to determine what our lessons are. With the ability to read energy patterns and to see beyond the illusion of surface appearances, it is much easier to help people identify and release their limiting thoughts, judgments, misperceptions and energy blockages, so they can reclaim their magnificence.

Chapter 2
The Soul's Journey of Learning

We're Here to Learn

Many people have the mistaken idea that Earth is a low level planet, like a kindergarten, where beginners come to learn and test themselves. Other people mistakenly believe they have been sent to Earth as a punishment. These ideas are the furthest thing from the truth.

Earth is a unique special place. It is a very challenging, advanced adventure park and place of learning where even masters come to test themselves. Beings come here to see if they can hold their balance and their commitment to achieving soul growth, and to attaining higher states of consciousness. The Earth experience offers the unique challenges and temptations of polarities, time, density and much more.

You would not have chosen to come to Earth unless your soul has specific lessons it wants to learn here. Souls choose to come to Earth for many reasons. Some choose to come for just a few lifetimes: to observe, to learn specific skills, to gain knowledge or to give certain gifts to this planet. Other souls choose a long-term learning experience here on Earth and might commit to hundreds if not thousands of Earth lifetimes. Every soul is eternal and enjoys a never-ending journey of expansion through infinite learning and growth, called *Soul Growth*.

For many of us, learning and expansion are the soul's goal while we're here on Earth. Earth is an adventure park and a place a soul can go to learn and gain experiences that will hopefully lead to greater knowledge, expertise, understanding and wisdom. Just as we have many levels of schooling for the *mind* here on Earth — from nursery school and kindergarten to high school, college and graduate schools — the universe offers its own version of schools for the *soul*. Our universe is home to a multitude of adventure parks and places of learning, and many more are available in other dimensions where souls can choose to attend and learn. In fact, many souls choose to do the majority of their learning in locations other than Earth.

Just like snowflakes, no two souls are the same. Each soul is unique and has a different soul path to follow. So, while some souls might go through similar experiences and tests, each one will process and interpret its experiences differently than any other soul will. Its insights and takeaways will be influenced by that soul's history and perspective.

When it comes to timing, a soul can choose to learn as quickly or as slowly as it wishes to. A number of factors can contribute to the agreements the soul makes about when to arrive on Earth and how frequently it wants to return here. And, since there's no urgency or race against time — in fact there's no time at all! — a soul can renegotiate or modify its soul agreement about when to come to Earth, how long it stays here, the lessons it learns and how often it returns here.

For a soul to learn its lessons, all of the necessary elements needed for learning have to be available. For example, if the soul wants to learn about leadership in war, it wouldn't make sense for it to incarnate during a time of peace. Similarly, all of the people the soul needs to interact with also need to be available during that lifetime.

If a soul is willing to face its issues, take full responsibility and learn its lessons, it progresses through its learning more quickly. If not, it will keep returning to Earth to repeat its lessons over and over until these lessons are mastered.

An infinite number of adventure parks, places of learning or training centers exist in multiple universes, realities and dimensions. Going to the wrong adventure park will not help you on your journey of learning. In fact, many environments and experiences might be totally useless for your soul's particular learning process. Just as it is very valuable to have a highly talented and experienced guidance counselor, coach or mentor on the Earth plane, it is extremely important that you have expert guidance and direction in both selecting and mastering your best learning and growth opportunities.

The Soul Continuum

The soul travels on an ongoing, never-ending journey of learning; the lessons it chooses to learn determine the direction that the journey takes. Every lifetime contributes its collection of learning experiences to a Learning Cycle of tests, trials and lessons. When the soul's lessons for a cycle are fully integrated, the soul moves on to a new cycle. This ongoing series of cycles of the soul is called the *Soul Continuum*.

Each learning cycle has major and minor themes for learning. As we gain experience and proficiency in a learning topic, we move on to other, more advanced aspects of the learning. When we gain the wisdom and knowledge we've committed to learn in our soul contract, we graduate and move on to other lessons.

As a soul gains experience in each lifetime, it progresses along its learning cycle, increasing its talents, abilities, skills and understanding. Each lifetime spent in learning moves it closer to mastery. For example, a soul that wants to learn math may progress from learning simple addition and subtraction to learning multiplication and division. Then the soul may choose to learn algebra. Then geometry. Then calculus. Then advanced calculus. With each and every expansion in learning, the soul moves closer and closer to attaining mastery in its chosen field.

Life Lessons and Themes

Before coming to Earth, while still in the spiritual realm, a soul will choose one, (or if appropriate, more than one) major and minor life lesson it wants to focus on. There are many lessons, themes and sub-themes that a soul might choose to master while here on Earth. Below are just a few possible ones:

COMMUNICATION

We all know people who find it difficult to verbally express themselves. Yet others, such as Rumi and Kahlil Gibran, through their internationally known writings and poetry, have touched the hearts and souls of millions of people. Rumi and Kahlil Gibran were in mastery lifetimes. By the time a soul enters into a mastery lifetime in communication, they have developed great skills in communicating, connecting and expressing themselves.

Having a communication theme in your life would involve lessons with verbal and non-verbal communication and it would embrace all levels: mental, physical, emotional and spiritual communication. The theme might include challenges with speaking, writing, non-verbal physical gestures and communicating using sounds, thoughts, feelings and emotions. It would embrace self-talk and self-communication too. Having a communication theme in your life might include sensitivity to the needs of yourself and others, self-expression, experiencing and expressing compassion towards yourself and others, sensitivity to intuition, energy and dreams, teaching, writing, communicating with plants, animals, insects and more. It might also include communicating with guides, teachers, your intuition, higher self and beings from different dimensions.

EMOTIONAL DEVELOPMENT

The lessons of a theme of emotional development include feeling, understanding, embracing, experiencing and expressing the full range of human emotions, emotional openness, receptivity, stability, integrity, sensitivity, balance, boundaries, discernment, flexibility, surrender of judgment, and willingness to feel and embrace all emotions appropriately without suppressing, limiting or judging them. The theme is also about developing the ability to connect and establish healthy intimacy.

POWER

The power theme includes understanding, accepting, embracing and using power appropriately. The soul might choose to learn to align its personal power with sacred divine power and keeping power in balance rather than over-powering or under-powering themselves and others. It might choose to learn about giving away its power, versus claiming and accepting its own personal power. The power theme can include the right use of will, creativity, manifestation, leadership and making choices. Lessons may include power in politics, power in the family, leadership during peaceful times, leadership during conflict, self-empowerment, power of presence, collaborative empowerment and creating abundance.

INDIVIDUATION

When an individuation theme is in play, the soul is choosing to learn about becoming healthy, whole and complete as an individual, as opposed to fitting in and being part of a family or group. This theme incorporates lessons in self-assertion, self-understanding, self-compassion, self-acceptance, self-support and trust of self to be free and to individuate. It might include learning to trust yourself and your choices, reclaiming your personal power, your willingness to be visible and trusting that you have the right to fulfill your personal wants, needs, feelings and desires. This theme also includes learning about personal entitlement, creativity and achieving personal goals, dreams and desires. With this theme, you will explore being true to yourself, and will be developing and refining thoughts, attitudes and beliefs about what it is to be an individual.

SERVICE

There are many forms of service. The theme of service includes unpaid and unrecognized selfless service to the community, to a religious group, to a religious order, to the entire planet through planetary service or to the universe through inter-dimensional service. The generous offering of time and talents in service to others is an important lesson.

Service can also be achieved by physically offering help or by meditating and praying for peace and positive outcomes. In some cases, others are aware of an individual's service and in other cases, no one else is aware of the individual's acts of service. Many consider the latter to be a higher form of service.

One of the challenges of this theme is to make sure that your reasons and motivation for doing service are pure and that you don't have any hidden expectations or agendas. Another challenging aspect of this theme is to make sure that you don't sacrifice yourself while serving others. All of these lessons are included in the theme of selfless service.

HEALING

The theme of healing involves issues of healing oneself and healing others on a mental, physical, emotional and spiritual level. It includes healing plants, animals, the land, the planet and the universe. The theme is also about healing thoughts, attitudes, beliefs, judgments, experiences, relationships, suffering, pain, trauma, past lifetimes and even future lifetimes. Healing can take the form of prayer, energy work, music, color, sound, art, humor, laughter and much more.

LOVE

Themes regarding love include love of self, love of others, romantic love, universal love, unconditional love, forgiveness, compassion, physical love, sensuality, sexuality, intimacy, love of beauty, love of nature, love of animals, love of travel, love of creativity, love of country, love of truth, family love, maternal love, paternal love, sibling love and love for a specific cause or calling.

Soul Qualities

A soul quality is a positive attribute of the human soul. When a human comes to Earth, she can have one or more soul qualities to support her on her Earth journey and/or she can choose a soul quality as a major theme for a life-learning lesson here.

Below is a partial list of the many soul qualities that we humans might choose for ourselves. To see the full list, see my website at www.michaelbradford.com where you can download it:

Abundance	Honesty	Purpose
Courage	Humor	Self-love
Creativity	Imagination	Sensuality
Discernment	Intuition	Spirituality
Freedom	Leadership	Will

Soul Agreements

Soul agreements and soul contracts are strong promises, commitments and agreements made from the highest level of the individual's soul. Soul agreements can be made individually to ourselves, with another being or with a group of souls. An individual soul agreement is created when a soul makes a commitment to incarnate in order to learn a specific lesson, fulfill a commitment or to heal a particular aspect of a past lifetime. While another person or a group of people, may be involved, he or she might not have any knowledge of the agreement.

A *Mutual Soul Agreement* is created when two people vow to incarnate together in order to complete unfinished business. Thirdly, a *Group Soul Agreement* is a commitment created when several individuals promise to incarnate together for the purpose of learning and healing. This agreement may also be for starting, expanding upon or completing a project already in progress.

Since a soul agreement is made from the soul level, fulfilling the contract is an important part of the reason the soul incarnates in this lifetime and it holds great importance to the evolution of the soul.

Agreements may be about performing some action, completing a task, or helping someone or a group of people to learn or accomplish something. Once a soul agreement or contract is made, there is usually a sense of urgency as well as a very strong conscious and unconscious energetic drive to complete it.

Since it holds great importance to the soul, when a soul agreement is not fulfilled, the person may experience intense feelings like hurt, anger, loss, failure, frustration, grief, disappointment, sadness, abandonment or betrayal.

If a soul attempts to assist another soul, but the person is not open, willing or receptive to receiving that assistance, conflict may easily erupt. The conflict may be expressed in disagreements or arguments, in one person feeling dominated and controlled, or either one feeling hurt, ignored, disappointed, unappreciated or betrayed. One person may feel driven to assist, while the other person, exercising her free will to accept or reject help, may feel imposed upon, pressured and disrespected. Inevitably, both people feel frustrated.

It is very important to keep your soul agreements in alignment with your soul evolution and your soul's purpose for incarnating in this lifetime. This is only one of the many reasons it is extremely important to have the help, guidance and support of others — such as intuitive energy healers, guides, teachers and coaches — who can identify your soul agreements and assist you in keeping them up to date.

Once you become aware of your soul agreement, you can review, update, modify, renegotiate or even cancel it. To facilitate the process, it is helpful to investigate how your soul agreement has served you, and how it serves the individual or group you made the soul agreement with.

As you learn, change, grow and evolve, your soul agreements and priorities will most likely change. For example, you may realize you need to let go of someone who is not willing or committed to learning, changing and growing. After all, it is not appropriate to sacrifice yourself or to allow yourself to be destroyed when you're trying to help another person.

Soul Contracts

Each soul makes a strong commitment to itself, in the form of a soul contract, to achieve its goals for learning in one of more areas. Its intention is to attain greater levels of proficiency that ultimately lead to mastery. When the soul achieves those goals, it moves on to other lessons.

We would not incarnate on Earth if we did not have a soul purpose for being here. Within each lifetime, our soul's purpose is to master the lessons we chose for ourselves. And each lifetime is different; the lessons depend on what we've committed to experiencing and learning in each lifetime.

Discovering, understanding and clarifying what your soul purpose is makes it a lot easier for you to understand your life challenges and your life direction.

No area of learning is more important, valuable or noble than any other. All lessons are equally important to the soul: it is all just learning. At higher levels of consciousness, the soul perceives no right vs. wrong, no good vs. bad, no higher or lower: everything is only learning. It is this ongoing soul growth, the learning and expansion that the soul longs for.

Understanding the Jigsaw Puzzle

If you are not consciously aware of the themes and challenges you've chosen to learn and master in your life, it will be far more difficult for you to understand the experiences you have attracted and are attracting. The greater your awareness and understanding of your soul's chosen themes, the better equipped you will be to face your tests and to select the best attitude to pursue in life. It also points the way to the easiest pathway forward for maximum soul growth and mastery in this lifetime.

Likewise, for anyone else to help, coach or mentor someone who's experiencing life challenges, it will help immensely to know what her soul has committed to learn and achieve in this lifetime and what her strengths, weaknesses and blind spots are.

As you discover more about yourself and your reasons for choosing to come to Earth, you will better understand your strengths, weaknesses and challenges in this lifetime. As you become more fully aware of your lessons and journey, each piece of the jigsaw puzzle fits into place and you can get deeper insight into how your current life has been affected by your past lives. You may also get a glimpse of your future lives.

Knowing where you are in your soul continuum can help you to recognize both your strengths and your challenges more clearly. The insight can also help you accelerate your learning process this lifetime. Understanding where you are on the continuum provides greater clarity, courage and confidence in your journey on planet Earth and beyond.

The Progress of a Soul

The progress of a soul on its journey from practice lifetime to mastery has many ups, downs and sideward movements; it is seldom, if ever, a straight line. There are even situations when a soul is only a few breaths away from achieving total mastery or even completion of all its Earth incarnations, but it judges itself or somehow feels unworthy. When this happens, the soul can energetically slip back and regress in its journey of learning. At such times, it would have to work through the unresolved issues that created the regression before it could continue forward.

Imagine a climber who is committed to climbing a very high snow and ice-covered mountain. The climber is constantly testing himself using all of his knowledge, skills and gifts to reach the summit. As he climbs upward, he may encounter many obstacles, like bad weather, lowered oxygen levels, falling stones, crevasses, avalanches, snowstorms and more. He may even have mental, emotional, physical or health challenges to contend with, too.

With all of the challenges he faces, he cannot progress in a straight line; instead, he is forced to zigzag up the mountain. Sometimes he even needs to descend to a lower elevation in order to avoid challenges. And if he were to fall or have an accident of some kind, he would have to improvise and recommit to achieving his goal of reaching the mountaintop in order to progress further.

The soul, on its journey to mastery, is much the same. Sometimes the soul is within sight of its goal, but then slips and has to retreat before reaching the summit, the knowledge, he pursues. The only solution is to seek lower ground, regroup and start again when possible.

While the path may be roundabout, remember that there are always tremendous opportunities for learning. It is said that a soul learns more from a failure than from a success. No matter what, it's always important to be compassionate and gentle with yourself and others. Whenever obstacles are encountered, it is best to honor yourself for being willing to be on the journey, and to maintain your focus on what you are learning and gaining.

Many different species and groups of beings are here on Earth, resulting in a very wide range of different types of consciousness, as well as different levels of consciousness. Within each species and group there may be a wide range of consciousness, from complete beginner to very aware enlightened beings.

Some beings, such as bodhisattvas, have already graduated from the Earth plane and have chosen to return to Earth to help, guide and teach. Others are helping as way-showers, healers and enlightened ones. These beings have come from many dimensions to assist us individually and to assist all of the Earth in its evolution.

Occasionally, even advanced beings fall into the traps of the Earth plane and have to go through the Earth learning cycles all over again. This is like slowly climbing to the top of a very large steep hill. And then, when you are within a dozen steps of the top of the hill, slipping, falling and rolling all the way down to the bottom of the hill. At that point, you have to start climbing all the way back up the hill again! Repeating and mastering these Earth learning journeys take a lot of discipline, commitment, time and energy.

A New Perspective

In the late 1980s, a friend of mine told me a story that challenged me to look at my life lessons from a new perspective. Whether the story is true or not, is not important. The lesson, however, is very important.

The story takes place on a remote uninhabited South Pacific island where a group of soldiers were taking part in a two-week jungle survival course. They were dropped off individually at various places around the island and had to survive on their own for two weeks.

When the soldiers were picked up, almost all of them had lost weight, were dirty, their clothes were torn and they looked tense and exhausted. But one soldier looked totally different from the others. When he was picked up, he was smiling, happy, relaxed, fully rested and his clothes were perfectly clean. He had even gained weight and had a nice suntan. His attitude and mindset were also very different from the other soldiers. Why?

In his mind, this soldier had decided that this survival course was actually the military giving him a well-earned paid vacation. So after he was dropped off, he immediately took off all of his clothes, neatly folded them and then went down to the beach and enjoyed himself.

For me, the questions and the lessons are clear. Do we choose to look at life as a struggle? Do we choose to fight and resist life? Do we choose to flow with life and allow life to support us? Do we let it take us to where we desire to go? Or are we resisting and fighting life and our learning lessons?

Chapter 3
The Soul's Interconnections

Soul Connections

Our souls create numerous connections from the moment we are born; most of us have families and extended families, we're part of religious and social groups, we live in communities and we are citizens of a country.

Similarly, our souls have connections with other *Soul Groups*, a group of souls that has specific talents, gifts, traits and focus. These multiple universal connections can extend to include galactic, intergalactic, dimensional, inter-dimensional and many other soul groups.

Each of us is a member of at least one *soul group* and has at least one *soul affiliation*, which is a loyalty, connection, trait or expression. We also make soul agreements and have soul lessons that we have agreed to learn and possibly master.

Kingdoms and Elements

Earth has many *Kingdoms* within which different types and levels of consciousness can be experienced and expressed. These kingdoms include the human, animal, mineral, plant, fairy, angelic and deva among others.

There are also *elements*, which are classified as the fundamental building blocks of nature. These include Earth, air, fire, water, wood, metal and ether.

There is no ranking or hierarchy among kingdoms to indicate that one is any better or more evolved than the next. Each kingdom and element is unique and has its own talents, gifts, lessons and evolutionary path. We humans can learn to call upon and access the power, wisdom, support and resources of the various kingdoms and elements for spiritual guidance, healing, assistance and support.

I have never observed a person seeming to progress upwards in an evolutionary path from one kingdom to another. To the contrary, I see each kingdom and element as a unique, complete and separate system; the consciousness and energy of those in the system evolve within it. At the same time, they can also interact with others within or outside of their system.

A being that has more than one connection between kingdoms and elements is considered a *Bridge Person*. A bridge person has access to the various kingdoms and elements he is connected to.

Someone who is passionate about helping animals may be a bridge person between the human kingdom and the animal kingdom. Although being human, this person may understand an animal's thoughts, feelings, emotions, wants, needs and desires even better than they understand those of humans, and may even be an animal whisperer.

Soul Affiliations

Each of us originates from a specific dimension, place or region in the universe and is affiliated with or is a member of, a specific group. A few of the soul affiliations that are represented on the Earth plane include:

- Angels and Angelic realms
- Archangels
- Extra-terrestrials (ETs)
- Inter-dimensional beings (from other dimensions)
- Inner-Earth beings
- Fairy kingdoms
- Devas
- Elementals

Angels and Archangels are described in many religions, and are most known. These are usually beings who incarnate to help Earth through challenging times or times of great change and expansion.

ETs are literally from outer space and other planets. People in this group like to look up at the night sky, watch the stars and often long for home.

Inter-dimensional beings originate from other dimensions.

Inner-Earth beings are attracted to rocks, stones, minerals and crystals

Devas are plant spirits. People who are affiliated with devas tend to love gardening. They buy plants and flowers for themselves and others.

Those affiliated with elementals are attracted to nature, the land, wind, storms, volcanoes, waterfalls, lakes, oceans, forests and the elements.

There are many other groups participating in the grand experiment on Planet Earth. All of them bring their unique gifts, qualities, lessons, teachings and blessings.

***

Peggy, a professional woman in her late 40s, had a passion for being around active volcanoes. She spent every vacation traveling the world visiting volcanoes. She had a strong soul affiliation with fire energy.

***

Judith, a psychic channel in her late 60s, was connected to the Deva community. She loved flowers and would spend hours in flower shops and botanical gardens being among "her people." When she was with the flowers, she felt at home and at peace. She frequently bought flowers for herself and for her friends, especially if they were going through a rough time.

Soul Groups

A *Soul Group* consists of souls who are interrelated and interconnected, who come from a similar place, have a similar focus and who belong to the same group organization or affiliation. They also have the same or similar talents, skills, goal and purpose.

When coming to Earth, these souls can come onto the planet at different locations, even different countries, which allows the soul group to have more of an international connection with their counterparts in other countries. At the other end of the spectrum, the soul group can choose to come to Earth at the same time, in the same region of a country and even at the exact same location. This allows the group members to grow up together, go to the same school together, learn together, work together as a team and co-create with each other to achieve specific objectives.

Sometimes large numbers of a specific soul group will incarnate together on Earth at the same time; during other times, just a few members do. It all depends upon the soul agreements of the group, as well as the conditions and learning opportunities available on Earth. There might be other times when none of the members of a particular soul group are present on Earth. This could be because they are not needed or there are no opportunities for them to learn and experience what they desire to learn and experience.

***

As the private session began, I sensed that John, a powerful warrior of the Light, had not been back on the Earth plane for over 25,000 years. This amazed me, as this was the longest time period between Earth lifetimes I had ever witnessed. When I told this to John, he immediately went into self-judgment, guilt, shame and blame, believing he had done something horribly wrong and was being punished for it. In his mind, he believed that he had been banished from Earth and therefore had not been allowed to come back sooner.

When I tuned into his energy and his soul records, it told a very different story. The reason he had not been allowed to return and incarnate on Earth any sooner was because the specific lessons his soul needed to learn had not been available on Earth yet, and the specific gifts he had to give the Earth were not needed until now. Any incarnation on Earth during the past 25,000 years would have been a complete waste of time for John's soul growth.

Once I explained all of this to John, it was as if a light bulb turned on for him. All of a sudden, he remembered the strong warrior of the Light that he was and also remembered why he incarnated this lifetime. He came to help the Earth to heal and to move into Light. With this new awareness, his energy shifted, he became lighter and he was able to release his undeserved negative self-judgment.

It is amazing how quickly people tend to judge themselves and to believe the worst, when in reality they did not do anything wrong or bad.

***

There are times when a small number of souls from a group incarnate together as part of a vanguard team to do a little reconnaissance: to establish contacts, lay a foundation for further connection and learn how humans think and act. They might check out how open and receptive we humans are at a particular time. They also might observe patterns, plant ideas or prepare the way so that other members of the group can come at a later time, when the Earth or humanity is going through challenging times, such as war or famine. They may also come to assist during times of expansion, exploration and rebirth, as they did during the Renaissance period.

***

One of my mentors told me that I am part of a vanguard team for the Yeshua Group and that very few of my soul group are on the Earth plane at this time. More members of the group will come at a later time, when the time is right. I'm told that the purpose of the Yeshua Group is to assist, support, teach, awaken, enlighten, heal and most of all, to help bring peace and harmony to Earth.

***

In 1983, I received a healing session that touched me deeply. The room was dim, music was playing softly and acupuncture needles were strategically placed in my third eye to open my awareness. All of a sudden, I saw, felt and experienced myself sitting on the back of a giant golden eagle.

Just as I was getting comfortable, giant curtains opened up in front of me, revealing the pitch-black night sky filled with many stars. With me on its back, the eagle took flight. As we flew in the night sky, a few bright lights joined in front of us and then, after a dozen seconds, slowly moved alongside us. Shortly thereafter, more bright lights arrived and arranged themselves in front of, alongside and behind us. Eventually, the Eagle and I were at the center of a bright diamond-shaped formation.

When I returned to the conscious state and shared what I saw with healer guiding me, I was told this was the symbol of the White Brotherhood.

Soul Bridges

Some of us are *Soul Bridges*, meaning we have more than one soul affiliation and so we can be loyal to more than one group of beings, energies and kingdoms at the same time. I feel intuitively that about 20% of the people on Earth are Soul Bridges — having at least one additional soul affiliation. I intuitively sense that only about 10% of the population has two or more soul affiliations.

The mission of a soul bridge is to assist the Earth by utilizing the combined energies, insights, talents, skills, awareness, abilities and support of their soul groups and soul affiliations. Their combined talents provide new unique perspectives for creating positive change and technological breakthroughs in society.

My mentors have told me that my soul connections are with the Extra Terrestrial and the Native American energies. They also told me that I am a Soul Bridge, since I connect the past (ancient wisdom and ancient healing techniques) with the future (future wisdom and future healing techniques). Each of us has one or more unique gifts that we bring to this planet.

Soul Resonance

When we hear someone's name, see their picture, meet them, hear their voice or even read something they wrote, we sometimes intuitively sense or feel an energetic pull, or a knowing that we need to connect with them. We might want to talk with the person, have a private session with them or study with them long term. Since this *Soul Resonance* is recognized by our feelings and intuition, as opposed to our intellect, it cannot always be understood, explained or quantified.

When our intuition senses danger, our reaction will often be to close down, protect ourselves and to pull away. When our intuition senses a positive opportunity, it calls upon us to have faith, trust, open up, risk, reach out, pay attention, take positive action and ask for what we really want.

Some time ago, while I was researching website layouts online, I was attracted to a healer's website. I was so moved that I sent her an email, saying, "Thank you for being on the planet! I just saw your website and felt like I had to drop you an email so we could connect!" Her reply was respectful yet cordial and the dialogue ended there. I wonder what the connection was that I sensed.

I strongly encourage people to reach out and explore their intuitive nudges and their connections to people, places and things. Our higher self, spirit and intuition often speak truth to us in soft whispers that the intellect cannot explain or understand.

There are times when we have opportunities to meet and connect with like-minded souls who are on similar missions. Since we all have free will, we have the option to reach out and connect with them or not. There will be times when one individual is open and receptive to connecting, while the other is not and so no connection is made. Connecting is a matter of listening, feeling, trusting, risking, having faith, timing, openness, willingness and preference.

On my travels around the world, I have met people who are extremely different from me and other people who are very similar to myself. All have been worthwhile connections. The more we stay present, open, receptive and aware, the more opportunities we will have to connect to the hearts and souls of others.

I trust that some of the people who read this book will resonate with my energy and the information I present here, and they will choose to connect with me on a deeper level as a fellow soul traveler, friend, healer, coach, teacher and possibly even as a mentor.

Soul Alliances

At times, different soul groups and those with different soul affiliations will join forces to help each other reach a common goal. These are called *Soul Alliances*. Alliances can be forged for the short term or long term, depending on what is desired or needed at the time. It is one of the reasons why certain groups can be found working together, despite how similar or different they are in nature. It is comparable to those times on Earth when a conflict or crisis occurs or when important international projects need to be completed: regardless of their differences, during times of need, people come together to help each other out.

Highly Evolved Groups

Throughout the universes and dimensions of our existence, there are many groups, councils, federations and organizations that are working together for the highest good of all concerned. These include the Councils and Tribunals of Light, of which the White Brotherhood, the Emerald Brotherhood and the Yeshua Group are members. These are just a few of the numerous groups that are members of the Councils and Tribunals of Light.

The Karmic Board, which operates similar to multiple judges in a courtroom, and oversees and administers the Laws of Karma, is another.

Please note that the term "Brotherhood" in the titles above does not refer to a gender in its meaning. Gender polarity does not exist anywhere else in the universe except Earth. Many spiritual people, including healers, intuitives and psychics, are members of one or more of these highly evolved groups.

Chapter 4
The Soul

What is Spirit?

The term *Spirit* — as used by Christian traditions in the term *Holy Spirit* and by some Native American spiritual traditions in *Great Spirit* — refers to the living, all encompassing, all-inclusive, universal Supreme Being. *Spirit* includes the big picture — all spirituality, all spirits and the entire spiritual universe.

The concept of Spirit relates to unified spirituality, universal consciousness and to the concept of a God or Deity. In Spirit, all separate individual energies, when connected with all other individual energies, form a greater interconnected collective unit. In other words, Spirit has an identity inclusive of, however separate from, all of its individual elements.

Spirit also has a consciousness and intellect greater than its elements; it has an ultimate, unified, non-duality awareness or force of life that combines and transcends all individual units of consciousness. The experience of this connection is the basis of spiritual belief.

The world famous American clairvoyant and healer, Edgar Cayce, also known as the Sleeping Prophet, channeled the following statement about Spirit:

Spirit forces are the animation of all life-giving, life-producing forces in animate or inanimate forces. Spiritual elements become corporeal when we speak of the spiritual body in a spiritual entity; then composed of spirit, soul and the super consciousness.

What is a Soul?

A soul is an individualized expression of Spirit. It is the eternal, everlasting spark of energy, light, consciousness and divinity that exists in all things and it connects everything in the universe. Some people believe the soul exists only in humans; however, from my firsthand experiences doing sacred ceremonies with indigenous people around the globe, I've come to understand and wholeheartedly accept that everything, including the land, as well as all animals, plants, trees, insects and even rocks have consciousness.

According to quantum physics — the theoretical basis of modern physics, which explains the nature and behavior of matter and energy on the atomic and subatomic level — we are all energetically part of an infinite whole. As such, everything in the entire universe is divinely interrelated and interconnected.

As with all matter and energy, a soul can neither be created nor destroyed. However, it can learn, change, transform and evolve.

Saying that humans are the only creatures in the universe that have a soul and consciousness is like saying that we Earth-based humans are the wisest, most evolved souls in all of creation. It also assumes that humans are at the absolute pinnacle of creation, within this universe, all universes and all dimensions. Considering the size of the universe and the distinct probability of the existence of extra-terrestrial, inter-dimensional and many other species, this seems extremely unlikely. It is time to look beyond ourselves so we can truly see and accept the bigger picture.

My experiences with indigenous people around the world have taught me that everything in the universe has consciousness. Every tree has a spirit and the forest as a whole has an overseeing Grandfather/Grandmother guardian spirit. As I travelled, studied and participated in sacred ceremonies, I learned to deeply respect all of life. Over the decades I have experienced energetic connections and intelligent communication with dolphins, mountains, clouds, animals, fish, plants, trees, insects, water, stones, air, fire and much more.

There are group spirits, guides and spirit animal helpers. I have become well aware of animal spirits, guardians and other spirit energies that are helping and assisting humans.

Some people have asked if humans were once minerals or animals. I cannot answer that, since I do not have first-hand experience. However, I don't believe that humans become animals or animals become human.

I believe that each energy of consciousness develops within its own kingdom. Hence minerals will develop and advance within the mineral kingdom, and do not move into the plant or the human kingdom. They may assist, however I do not believe they evolve into the other kingdoms.

Shamans and medicine people will call forth and invoke the energies and the attributes of specific plants, minerals, animals and other energies to assist people, and to increase their abilities and power. However these are strictly helpers and are not a part of a person's soul.

Regarding the hierarchy of intelligence, I believe that everything has its own unique form and level of intelligence. I know that plants, animals, birds, turtles and others are all part of the whole. As such, each brings a special sacred frequency and vibration to Earth. To me, no plant, animal or human is more sacred than any other energy. In my heart and soul, I know that we are all one and we are here to learn to love, honor, respect, support and help each other.

The Lakota Sioux (Native American) people use the term, *Aho Mitakuye Oyasin*, which translates to "*All My Relations*." The Native Americans and all indigenous cultures consider all of creation to be both connected and related to us. The native people also say that if all the plants and animals died off or were killed, that they would be very sad and lonely without their relatives.

Where Do Souls Originate?

Some believe that all souls originate from the mind of God/Spirit and are then dispersed throughout the universe. Regardless of where they come from, many souls live in many dimensions and in many physical as well as non-physical universes.

Souls come to the Earth plane from other parts of this physical universe, as well as from other universes, other dimensions, other realities and other realms of consciousness. There are Universal Laws governing the Earth and other realms. As long as these Universal Laws are honored, respected and are not violated, such as the Law of Non-interference, souls are allowed to choose to attend the various places of learning that these universes provide.

Made up of energy and consciousness, the soul does not have solid, physical material mass. It is purely energetic in nature, usually vibrating at a very high frequency.

There are a numerous opinions about where the soul lives. Some say it resides in your heart; some say it resides in your brain; some say it resides within the vitality of the solar plexus system with the gland of the medulla oblongata; others say it resides throughout the entire physical body. I believe the soul is located in your heart area and is a key part of your life-force energy.

Some energetically sensitive people can sense and even see the soul as it comes into the embryo or fetus. Depending upon what experience the soul chooses to experience, it will enter the human body at some time between conception and birth.

The Soul Leaves the Body at Death

Some spiritual people can sense or even see the soul as it leaves the physical body at the time of transition or death. People who have seen the soul release from the physical body say it looks like an energetic haze, a mist or a puff of smoke.

At the time of death, there is also a very slight weight loss, which scientifically proves some form of energy matter is lost, even though there is no visible or physical manifestation.

The weight loss at the time of death has been scientifically verified by medical experiments. Dr. Duncan MacDougall an early 20th-century physician in Massachusetts sought to measure the mass that was lost by humans when the soul departed the body. He measured the weight change of six patients at their moment of death. His results indicated that there was a weight loss of three-fourths of an ounce, a measure recently popularized as 21 grams.

How Does A Soul Evolve?

As a soul challenges itself and as it risks, learns lessons and passes tests, it expands. Its frequency and vibration increase. It becomes lighter, less dark and dense, and it gains more light. When this happens, the soul moves up the ladder of evolution, and enters into higher and higher realms of consciousness.

If the soul avoids learning, avoids taking responsibility or fails lessons, its frequency and vibration decrease, and it becomes denser and heavier. Its light becomes dimmer, too. When this happens, the soul can slip down the ladder of spiritual evolution, and descend to lower and lower levels of consciousness.

It's important to remember that soul learning does not happen along a straight line. What may appear to you to be a slip down the ladder may actually be a detour or divergence, which will soon lead you to tremendous positive upward movement.

I have become violently ill just shortly after a transformative experience a number of times in my life. It has happened when I went swimming with wild dolphins in Key West, Florida and the Red Sea (Egypt), and when I swam with manta rays and spent time with the Komodo Dragons in Indonesia. I had a number of symptoms, including high fever, vomiting, diarrhea, severe headaches, muscle aches and joint pains.

Just after swimming with the wild dolphins for the first time in 1991, I had a 104° F fever for almost two weeks. Even though the doctors did extensive blood work and other testing on me, they could not find anything wrong with me. For over 20 years, I thought I had a serious health issue, like Lyme's disease or some other rare exotic health challenge.

Only recently I learned that these experiences were not severe negative health challenges or low points in my life after all. In fact, they were extremely positive periods of accelerated soul growth, where I had burned off a tremendous amount of negative karma, grew rapidly spiritually and broke through to higher levels of consciousness.

Everything we experience is a learning process; it is the long-term results that are most important, and not just short-term gains or losses. Experiences that appear to be less than positive can provide extremely valuable lessons for the soul. There are even times when the soul can knowingly choose to go into the darkness — into lower level energies, such as extreme depression, alcoholism, drugs or other addictions — to learn incredibly valuable lessons that will eventually allow it to make a very positive, quantum leap forward in its long-term evolutionary growth.

This is why it is so important that we suspend all comparisons, labels and judgments about others and especially about ourselves. Regardless of what the outward appearance are, we are all always Spirit/God creating!

There is an old profound statement that says, *"What doesn't kill you, will make you stronger!"* Everything we experience is a golden opportunity for learning, changing, growing, healing and spiritually expanding.

***

Robert, a very psychic and spiritual police detective I met in Europe, shared with me that he was amazed when he observed the energy fields of a number of the hit men he arrested. He discerned that they were actually very highly evolved spiritual beings. This experience raised a lot of questions in Robert's mind, because their profession as hit men who were responsible for murdering people and their high level of spiritual evolution seemed to reflect diametrically opposed values — at least according to his perceptions and value system.

Similarly, according to some with spiritual vision, a number of the hangmen and operators of the French guillotines in the past were very spiritual beings who were, in secret, helping the souls of those who were killed to release their trauma and move more easily into the spirit world.

Perspective is Everything

Everything is relative to your perspective. Everything depends on the way you look at things, your life lessons, attitudes, beliefs, judgments and prejudices — and ultimately on your level of consciousness.

Imagine a graph that measures the evolution of human consciousness on the vertical axis, from 0% to 100%. If your level of awareness were notated on it, say at the 25% level, then the 75% of people who are higher than you from an evolutionary standpoint will appear to be lighter, more aware and more evolved than you. When you look at the 25% of people who are represented on the graph below you, they appear to be darker, denser, less aware and less advanced than you.

When you progress on your journey of consciousness, to an 80% position for example, then only the 20% of the people ahead of you will seem to be lighter, more aware and more advanced than you, while the 80% of the people behind you on the journey will seem darker, denser, less aware and less evolved than you.

In both scenarios, the souls you observed had not changed — only your perception and perspective has changed.

The lesson here is to avoid comparing yourself to others and judging people, especially yourself. Simply seek out people you feel comfortable with, who you can relate to and who you resonate with. Accept the learning path of other people and allow others to do their own thing — as long as they are not imposing their will upon you or hurting you. Please remember that your soul's journey is not a race or a competition.

Life and evolution are ever-changing. Everyone learns, changes and grows at his or her own rate. All of us, regardless of our perceptions and prejudices, are in our perfect place, doing our perfect thing, living our perfect reality and learning our perfect lessons, until we choose to change and do something else. In other words, we simply are where we are at any given time — and so is everyone else.

In order to change one's life's circumstances, a person has to want them to change. No one can make anyone do anything that they do not want to do or choose to do. Even if they did manage to start to make modifications, the change would not last. This is especially true when the change is done solely to please others.

Perhaps even harder to recognize is that any time you attempt to control someone, get love from them or change them in any way, you are behaving in a dysfunctional way.

There is a Native American story I like that says it well:

Be like the Eagle. Close your eyes and fly as high as you possibly can. When you get there, allow yourself to do swirls and twirls, and when you are at your absolute most magnificence, open your eyes, celebrate and enjoy the other eagles around you. Do not reach down to pull anyone up to your level and do not reach up to pull anyone down to your level. When you accomplish this, you will be truly happy.

***

When I was teaching a workshop in Bristol, England many years ago, one of the men on my workshop support team would interrupt and yell out the words, "Horse water!" from time to time. After about the third time he did this, others in the workshop asked him what his outbursts were all about. His reply was classic. He said, "Michael is wasting time with that person. You can lead a horse to water, but you can't make it drink! This person is not ready or willing to benefit from what Michael has to offer them. For that reason, I'd like Michael to stop wasting the time of the group and move onto the next person!"

I've since learned that there's more to that story, though. That is: while you can't force a horse to drink, you can definitely make the horse thirsty by putting salt in his oats!

Chapter 5
Types of Earth Lifetimes

The Soul Continuum

Within the soul continuum, every new cycle of learning begins with a *practice* lifetime and progresses through countless lifetimes towards a *mastery* lifetime. This progression, from practice to mastery, may take dozens, hundreds or even thousands of lifetimes.

The soul may choose many cycles of learning and achieve many mastery lifetimes within its agreed upon continuum before it completes everything it wanted to learn on Earth. When all these lessons are learned and mastered, the soul is ready to graduate, move on and leave the Earth. Upon completion, the soul may then choose to go to other places of learning in other universes and dimensions, or it can choose to come back to Earth with an entirely new set of goals.

Sometimes a *mastery* lifetime is also a *completion lifetime* — the completion of all the learning on the Earth plane that the soul has committed to learn. Depending upon what the soul has committed to achieving, it may experience a single mastery lifetime or many hundreds of mastery lifetimes before completing and graduating from its Earth visit. Once the soul has achieved a mastery lifetime or a completion lifetime, it will have a new set of choices to make.

For example, if a soul is in a practice lifetime in a cycle of learning self-expression, it will be given many opportunities to learn to express itself. Later, in an *integration* lifetime the soul may be required to learn to balance its self-expression with the needs of a community, group or family. Then, during a mastery lifetime, it will have many opportunities to perfect, refine and possibly teach others self-expression.

Once the soul has mastered its self-expression cycle, it can choose to return to Earth again for a new cycle of learning or it can go to another place of learning, either in this universe or in another dimension. If it comes back to Earth, it can refine its education in self-expression by selecting another theme like s*elf-expression in acts of service* or *self-expression in acts of power*. Once the new theme is selected, the soul would begin again with a practice lifetime in its new continuum and move towards mastery within the new theme.

At the end of each lifetime, a soul meets with its guides and teachers for a *Past-Life Review*. At such a time, the soul, with the assistance of the guides and teachers, reviews its progress, recalls what it has learned, recognizes what it did well, is made aware of where there is room for improvement and evaluates what areas it may choose to improve. Please be aware that this review is a gentle, kind, loving, respectful process where understanding and compassion are present.

All of the tests, trials and grades that the soul has experienced are recorded on the soul's cosmic report card. Please be aware that perfection and speed are not critical here. Each soul has as long as it wants and needs to learn its lessons.

Practice Lifetimes

A *practice lifetime* is the first lifetime in a new continuum. In a practice lifetime, an individual chooses among thousands of possible topics — such as music, power, math, love or creativity — as long as he has no prior experience or expertise in that area. In the practice lifetime the individual is completely free to practice, explore and discover. Like a newborn, wide-eyed child, he is expected to be curious about exploring his new world.

The only requirement in a practice lifetime is for the individual to stay open, receptive, sincere, curious and aware of his new surroundings and experiences. It is a time to practice and play with one's unexplored life experiences.

The most challenging aspect about a practice lifetime is that it often comes after a mastery lifetime, when the individual had achieved perfection and mastery in some other area of learning. When this happens, a soul can come in with unrealistically high expectations, get frustrated easily and then be hard on herself when she cannot perform and master the new lessons easily, instantly and perfectly the first time she attempts something new.

The truth is that there are no measurements, tests or grades in a practice lifetime. Just like nursery school, the soul is free to play and explore without being graded; it gets credit just for showing up and experimenting. The only measurement is whether the person is willing to explore and gain learning in their new area of interest. Patience, self-compassion and a sense of humor go a long way. The more the individual learns to relax into her new learning experiences and to laugh at herself, the easier her life will be.

As a soul gains experience through a series of lifetimes, it will move on to more advanced lifetimes. Practice, patience, curiosity and self-compassion are very important: a new skill or way of being may take dozens, if not hundreds of lifetimes to learn and master.

* * *

Frank, a French man in his early twenties, was confused about his sexuality and his relationships with women. In his private session, he shared that he had many women friends who adored him. Although he felt totally comfortable with women as friends, when it came time to having sexual relations with them, he felt ashamed and guilty. He was not able to feel comfortable with or enjoy a healthy sexual relationship with any woman and he wanted to know why not.

I looked at Frank's soul path and saw that Frank was in a practice lifetime and he had made the commitment to learn about male consciousness. He had just completed a mastery lifetime, which was the culmination of his choosing to spend many lifetimes learning about being a woman and about feminine consciousness. His most recent previous lifetimes were spent in a female body mastering learning about the ways a woman thinks, feels, communicates and expresses herself in the world.

To complicate matters further, he had spent these recent lifetimes in religious orders where celibacy was required. As a result, Frank was used to being celibate and to relating to women as sisters rather than as lovers. Adding even more to his current challenges, as a woman in previous lives, he had judged masculine energy as inferior and bad.

Frank successfully completed his progression from practice lifetime to mastery lifetime by learning about how a woman thinks, feels and acts. Then, Frank's soul made the choice to learn about male consciousness and masculine energy. It seemed to him that everyone else — men and women alike — knew the rules on how to be a man; but he just didn't feel like he had a clue about it. He felt confused when he was in the company of men who seemed more experienced and comfortable being a man than he did. He was absolutely correct: he did not have a clue how to express himself as a male.

Frank was relieved to learn that he had not done anything wrong. He also realized how much courage it took to be in a male body after living so many lifetimes as a woman in religious orders and judging the male energy so harshly. As his session progressed, he began to understand that he was not betraying his spirituality or his women friends — his "sisters" — by being affectionate and sexual. With this new information, he was able to breathe a sigh of relief and relax. Perfection was not the goal — only exploring without judgment.

Soul Space

Believe it or not, the soul can get some down time in between lifetimes. Whenever it wants to, a soul can take a break and spend time in what is called *Soul Space*. Soul space, located outside of the Earth dimension, is a place where an individual soul can rest, relax, recharge, gather strength, heal and recover. Although it is not a holiday or a vacation exactly, it does give the soul a chance to catch its breath, integrate and rejuvenate. This typically happens after a soul experiences a traumatic or exhausting lifetime on Earth.

In soul space, the soul has no physical body. It is pure energy, connected to the Akashic records, a depository of all knowledge. In soul space, a soul's thoughts and desires are manifested instantaneously. Life and time are not linear as they are on Earth; everything is multidimensional. There is also no need for learning since everything is already known.

Time spent in soul space may be the equivalent to one or even a few Earth lifetimes. When a soul has regained her clarity, energy and strength, she returns to the Earth plane to resume her lessons. Not surprisingly, when souls return to the Earth plane from soul space, they sometimes seem distant, disoriented and disconnected to themselves and those around them.

* * *

Rebecca, an intelligent 14-year-old, was not happy in school. She felt like a misfit. She was bored, depressed and in danger of flunking out of school. Although she understood her schoolwork, she had little interest in doing her homework assignments and even less interest in taking her tests. She was challenging and rebellious, and often asked her teachers questions that they could not answer. They labeled her a troublemaker.

Rebecca longed to be back home, which, according to her, was somewhere other than Earth. During Rebecca's session, she learned that she had been in soul space for the last two Earth lifetimes and that she had chosen to come to Earth this time around to learn how the Earth functions. She learned that she's here to give her gifts to this planet, when the time was right.

Rebecca settled down after she gained a better understanding of her life mission and purpose. She had an easier time concentrating and began to do better in school. Her parents helped her to change schools so she could get the attention and support she needed. Soon, she began to feel more at ease with life on this Earth plane.

Somersault Lifetimes

Sometimes a soul will bounce back and forth between two extremely different lifetime themes and *"Somersault"* between lifetimes. These extremes might be between abuser and healer, monk and playboy, being very rich and being very poor, perpetrator and victim, warrior and peacemaker, extrovert and introvert, leader and follower and so on.

Somersault lifetimes are concerned with honoring, respecting, bringing together, blending and healing two extremely different attitudes, beliefs and energies. In this situation, a soul has harshly judged a certain polarity as being bad or wrong in one or more lifetimes, and is doing his best to balance his energy and heal the polarity. He may have several lifetimes where the polarities are experienced before he can progress into an integration lifetime where he is able to fully heal his energetic split. Once this is achieved, the soul feels more peace and harmony.

* * *

Steve was a businessman in his early 50s. He was overweight, had low self-esteem and a habit of sabotaging himself and feeling responsible for the happiness of others. He had worked hard over the years and had experienced a number of business successes and failures. He described himself as being a victim.

Steve complained that he never seemed to be able to achieve or maintain success. Although he had attained great success for short periods of time, he lost it all and consistently ended up deeply in debt. Turns out, Steve's soul agreement in this lifetime is to learn about self-control, personal power and the right use of will.

It was easy to see that Steve had bounced back and forth between lifetimes of having absolute power and not having any power. In this lifetime, he enjoyed being in control and welcomed any opportunity to demonstrate his prowess and overpower others. It was time for Steve to forgive himself and to bring the two polarities into harmony and balance. Once he does that, his rollercoaster ride will end and he will be able to achieve the success he so desperately wants.

* * *

Sharon, a healer in her mid-thirties, had weak energetic boundaries and showed up like an emotional sponge: energetically picking up and absorbing the physical symptoms, feelings, pain, anxiety and frustrations of the people around her.

In the past, Sharon had been emotionally shut down, aloof, independent, self-sufficient and emotionally detached from herself and others. She had also judged others for having the very emotions she wouldn't let herself feel and be vulnerable to.

Integrating her two polarity lifetimes allowed Sharon to find a more centered place where she could embrace greater self-compassion, and to be in more balance and harmony within herself. The process helped eliminate unhealed reactions within her and, as a result, helped her to stop picking up the emotional static around her.

Catch-Up Lifetimes

Catch-up lifetimes often follow one of more practice or somersault lifetimes and help the soul make up for lost time with their soul agreements. Perhaps a soul has avoided or fallen behind in the lessons she's chosen for herself. In a catch-up lifetime, she can work to catch up on those lessons. These lifetimes can often be intense and challenging since they might have added challenges that help the soul make up for lost time.

Please remember that it is the soul itself, not any other being or outside influence, which chooses the speed at which it desires to learn, change and grow.

* * *

In his late 50s, Peter had married a woman he didn't love in order to gain entry into a community. He wasn't happy in his marriage nor did he feel he was being authentic within the community.

In practice lifetimes, Peter had started to gain experience about being a loyal member of a group. Now in this catch-up lifetime, his soul purpose is to explore his personal freedom and to individuate from the collective. His soul commitment in this lifetime is to learn more about being true to his personal wants, needs, desires, feelings and goals.

Although Peter wanted to be true to himself and to his soul agreements, he also wanted to be loyal to his community, and did not want to hurt or disappoint anyone. Whenever he considered doing anything for his own interests, he was overwhelmed with shame and guilt.

The key to his healing was for him to be totally open and honest with everyone, to let go of control and wanting to be accepted, and to trust the process and to support his own soul destiny. His soul was demanding this level of self and group honesty and would not support him in betraying himself this lifetime.

* * *

Paula worked as a social worker helping people who were mentally and emotionally challenged. She was caring, sensitive, empathetic and was instinctively aware of other people's needs. Helping, serving and taking care of others came easily and naturally to her, however she did not have a clue how to identify and to take care of her own wants, needs, desires and dreams.

Paula had dedicated a number of lifetimes to serving others. Her soul's purpose this catch-up lifetime was to claim her own sense of self-entitlement, and to follow her own heart and desires. It didn't matter which interests or subjects she pursued, only that she follow her own inner longings and desires.

Integration Lifetimes

Integration lifetimes are focused on healing unresolved polarity splits. They usually follow other incarnations where a person has led an "either/or" polarity existence. In many ways, this lifetime has the dual focus of honoring, healing and merging the two diametrically opposed ways of being. By honoring them equally and bringing them together, the objective is to come to a middle ground and create a more peaceful, balanced and harmonious way of living. It is definitely a complex challenge.

* * *

Priscilla felt a profound emptiness even though she had a successful business career, a happy marriage and wonderful children. As she was an accountant in her early 50s, those around her expected her to be practical, logical and analytical. So she relied heavily on her left-brain intellect and largely ignored and doubted her intuition.

Priscilla's challenge in this integration lifetime is to trust her intuition as much as her well-developed intellect. In previous lives, when she had trusted her intuition, she had ignored her intellect. Now it is time for her to honor both faculties equally and to bring them into balance and harmony.

* * *

Kevin was living a life seemingly out of control. An entrepreneur in his early 30s, he felt like he vacillated between two different people with two extremely different personalities. He alternated between being the life of the party on the one extreme and withdrawing from social experiences on the other.

Kevin is in an integration lifetime and his soul purpose this lifetime is to honor and integrate both of these polarities without judging himself.

Recovery Lifetimes

Recovery lifetimes are dedicated to healing, resolving, reclaiming and re-investing in life and living. It is as if the person had slipped on a banana peel and fallen. Now the soul's main job is to get up, brush itself off, recommit to life, living and learning its lessons, and move forward on its journey.

Recovery lifetimes are often about healing traumas, addictions, losses and bad judgments. Many times, there is a strong karmic pattern that must be broken and released for a meaningful recovery to take place. A recovery lifetime is often intense: the soul encounters challenging people from this and other lifetimes. Traumatic themes and events from past lifetimes are revisited. Even if the souls or energies from previous lives are not available to help in the recovery this time around, the soul will attract other people and situations with similar discordant energies and patterns to push against.

$$* * *$$

Jane, an independent attorney in her mid 30s, desperately wanted to settle down, get married and raise a family. But she questioned whether being married and having a family was in alignment with her soul purpose for this lifetime. She felt deep down in her soul that she was a healer, but anytime she thought about using her abilities, she had panic attacks and feared she would have to sacrifice something extremely important to her in order to follow her calling.

In a previous lifetime, Jane had been a famous female healer who was married with three children. Because she refused to allow the government to control her, they kidnapped her children and threatened to kill them if Jane did not obey their wishes. When she could not locate her children by using her skills as a psychic and healer, she judged herself and fell into a deep depression.

In this lifetime, Jane was protecting herself in several ways: by staying single, by not having children, and by not claiming her abilities as a psychic and healer. This level of defense was unconscious, but it was seemingly effective in protecting herself, her partner and her children.

As part of her recovery process, she forgave herself for not being able to protect her children in that lifetime. She also made the commitment to strengthen the relationship with the man she was dating and signed up for some classes on healing.

* * *

Richard, a business coach in his mid-forties, had challenges with making commitments and following through. While he was very good at starting projects, he rarely completed them. In a previous lifetime, Richard had made a soul commitment to dedicate himself to the priesthood. Just as he was about to take his final vows, a messenger arrived to tell him that his father was dying, and to ask him to go home to take care of his father and the family.

A dutiful son, Richard left to take care of his ailing father and by doing so, he walked away from his soul commitment to the priesthood. Although it was his soul purpose in that lifetime to dedicate himself to the priesthood, because of his family commitments, he never achieved it. When Richard learned that his guilt for getting so close to his goal but not achieving it was unconsciously sabotaging him in this lifetime, he understood why he wasn't able to accomplish his goals in this lifetime. As a result of this realization, he was able to make a shift.

To heal the pattern, Richard realized he had to heal the trauma he felt when he abandoned his soul purpose in the other lifetime. He knew that to fully heal, he would have to commit to completing his projects and dreams, and to trust that they would come to fruition.

Mastery Lifetimes

Each soul spends many lifetimes practicing and perfecting what they wish to learn within their chosen theme. Eventually, each soul will achieve a lifetime where it becomes very proficient at the lessons it committed to learn. At such a time, the individual is at the top of her game, yet continues to become even more proficient and efficient at her chosen skills.

Please be aware that attaining a level of mastery within one area of learning doesn't necessarily mean that all other areas of someone's life are at the same level. Just like with more mundane skills in life — such as cooking, mechanics, music or accounting — someone may have exceptional skill in that area, but not in others.

* * *

Marcus was a sculptor who found it difficult to maintain long-term relationships with women. Looking over his life, he had experienced numerous relationships; however, he could not seem to allow his heart to open fully and commit to a long-term relationship. He felt guilty that women were less important to him than his work.

When Marcus realized that he had made a soul commitment to himself to become one of the best sculptors in the world during this lifetime, he laughed. Deep inside he knew that this was his lifetime to shine. For many lifetimes he had majored in creative expression through clay, color, fabric and even metals.

When he learned that he was in a mastery lifetime, Marcus gave himself permission to do what his heart longed for. He also gave himself permission to attract a woman who would understand his passion for art and would support his professional goals.

* * *

Ann, a top executive in her early 30s, held a very important corporate position. She did her job so easily that her co-workers felt intimidated by her abilities and competence. Even though she appeared to be happy, however, Ann was feeling held back and suffocated by her current job.

When Ann learned that she was in a mastery lifetime to teach creativity, she smiled. She realized she had made a soul commitment to teach others about creativity and wanted to help others to develop their creative skills. Knowing she could not achieve her goals within her current corporate position, Ann quit and started her own company, which focused on teaching creativity to children, young adults and corporate clients.

Completion Lifetimes

A *completion lifetime* is the last Earth lifetime that a soul experiences within their agreed upon continuum, marking their graduation from the Earth plane. This occurs after the successful completion of one or more mastery lifetimes. After graduation, the soul has a number of choices. It can choose to return to Earth to learn additional skills in an entirely new continuum, or it can choose to gain experiences in other places of learning in other dimensions and universes. It may also choose to return to Earth as a spiritual guide or teacher to help others. In Buddhism, such a person is called a bodhisattva.

A completion lifetime is marked by a sense of urgency and the tendency to want things to be perfect. The soul often has an urge to clear up unresolved and unhealed karma from the past, so it can move forward with as little baggage as possible. It will also incorporate many of the resources and lessons from many previous lifetimes.

A soul in a completion lifetime will attract situations, places, people and relationships that had challenged them in their past so that it can heal and complete as much unfinished business as possible. It may also attract others with similar patterns who still need healing or are engaged in completing their unfinished events.

* * *

David, a man in his 50s, was in his last lifetime on Earth. Looking at his astrological chart made many people cringe because it was clear to them that David had chosen to take on five lifetimes' worth of unfinished karma in order to finish up his learnings on this planet. As a result, David was faced with many more intense challenges than most other people. Seeing his chart and understanding why he was experiencing these intense challenges helped David to better understand his process. It also helped him to stop blaming himself and to stop looking for reasons why he was not experiencing the life that "normal" people experience.

* * *

Henry retired from his position as vice president of a successful multi-million dollar business. After retiring, he started to mentor young adults who were starting their own business ventures and began volunteering as a consultant for a local non-profit community group. In addition to those efforts, he was also spending large chunks of time with his two grandchildren. Even though he was accomplishing a lot, Henry felt frustrated and unfulfilled, and he had a burning desire to contribute more.

Looking at Henry's placement on his soul continuum, it was not surprising to discover that he was in a completion lifetime. His soul commitment was to use all of the knowledge and expertise he had gained throughout his many lifetimes to teach others. Realizing that he was right on track and in alignment with his soul purpose, Henry relaxed and quickly made peace with his pressing desire to teach others and to spend quality time with his grandchildren. He realized that he did not have to choose one over the other: he could enjoy both.

* * *

Paula was a computer programmer in her late 50s. She was feeling frustrated and unsatisfied in her relationships even though she had successfully attracted caring, devoted partners for most of her life. According to her spiritual guides, she was in a completion lifetime and had made a soul commitment to heal painful relationships from the past.

Although Paula did not believe in past lifetimes, she admitted that she felt like her lovers were somehow familiar to her. With this new information from her guides, she decided to invite a healing quality into her existing relationships. She was also reminded to be kind and gentle with herself, and with others.

As a result of this guidance, Paula stopped looking for the ideal relationship and started to accept and appreciate herself, and the relationships she had. She also started to ask herself how she could be more compassionate, kind and loving towards herself and her partner. Understanding that she was in a completion lifetime allowed her to better understand and accept herself, and the relationships she attracted.

The Soul's Infinite Journey

Soul learning and soul expansion is not a destination. It is a never-ending journey that will continue until the end of time. As you take your next step on your eternal journey, you may wish to smile, relax, breathe and enjoy yourself as you proceed through your rich landscape of lessons.

Chapter 6
The Challenges of Being Human

Ego Personality Versus Soul

For many of us, both our ego and our personality are in an ongoing life-and-death power struggle with our soul. Your soul is always positively encouraging you to risk, learn, change, grow and expand your awareness. It is not concerned about money, power, status, earthly rules, looking good or being right. It is only concerned with completing your soul agreements and enhancing your soul growth. From a soul perspective, risking and being energetically present, open, honest and vulnerable are considered great achievements.

On the other hand, both your ego and your personality have a vested interest in keeping you trapped in old paradigms and maintaining control over you so that you stay stuck, focused on looking good, being right and fitting in. Your ego and personality cannot and will not admit that they don't know something or that they're wrong about anything. They will make up stories and create a million excuses rather than risk asking for help and allowing others to help them. From the ego and personality perspective, being energetically present, open, honest, vulnerable and asking for help are seen as weaknesses — possibly even life threatening — and something to be avoided at all costs.

This is especially true for those who were raised in a dysfunctional family or in an environment where they did not feel safe. In such cases, many children survived by withdrawing deep inside themselves and developing a false sense of self, otherwise known as a *Mask* or a *Persona*.

For example, some people consciously know that they are arguing, fighting and resisting a situation they feel uncomfortable with, yet they are too afraid to admit they don't know what to do about it or that they need help. Their subconscious programming tells them: since they didn't feel safe and couldn't trust their own family, how could they ever trust anyone else? So they may withdraw, keep quiet and implode or at the other extreme, rebel, resist, be angry, fight, act out and explode.

This dilemma can sometimes cause a *Shame Bind*. A shame bind occurs when a person knows he needs help, but he is too embarrassed and ashamed of his actions to face and admit what's really going on. He may consciously or even unconsciously resist or fight anyone who tries to get close to him, help him, love or support him. He believes that he can't trust anyone to get close to him.

Some people are strong enough to suppress and control their painful memories and experiences, at least for a while. They may be able to have fairly healthy interactions with others, at least superficially. But when they feel pressured or when they start to really trust and relax, it can become too challenging for them to maintain that surface control. Instead, old suppressed memories including anger, hurt, fears, pain, anxiety and unresolved traumas can bubble up to the surface and contaminate or even destroy any number of relationships — including friendships, romantic relationships and business partnerships.

The sooner we resolve our deep-seated traumas and pains, the sooner we can learn to love, honor, respect and support ourselves, and to establish meaningful, healthy relationships with others. The only way to permanently and completely resolve these kinds of issues is to identify them, face them and heal them at the deepest level of your being. Facing these kinds of issues takes tremendous courage. Having a highly experienced intuitive guide and coach can assist you to quickly identify and release your deepest core issue, thus allowing you to greatly reduce or eliminate a lot of time, stress, confusion, trauma and expense as you transform them. With the techniques I have developed, many people have been able to accomplish profound healing in just a few sessions.

* * *

When I first met Phyllis, a Dutch woman in her late 50s, the energy between us was so negatively charged with discordant energy and static that it felt like we were in an energetic war zone. This negative energy was so strong that it actually made audible crackling sounds and was physically painful to both of us. On the surface, Phyllis appeared very calm and serene, however the energy between us was so scrambled that it was impossible for us to be around each other. As a result, we parted ways and lost contact.

Over 10 years later, while in meditation, her guides and intuition instructed her to contact me for help regarding a health challenge she was facing. Based on our previous interaction, I was the last person on Earth she would have consciously contacted. While I usually only have to work with a client once or twice, Phyllis's case was very different. Because of the severe childhood trauma she was carrying and her extremely high level of distrust of men, her protective ego and personality defenses would not let go easily.

It took about six sessions over a few months for Phyllis to gain the courage to face her childhood pain and to feel safe enough to stay energetically present with me. During this time, Phyllis started to change, becoming more present, internally calmer and more peaceful. Her health also dramatically improved.

It helped when I told Phyllis that she was in an integration lifetime and explained what that meant. As she allowed herself to trust that she was seen, heard, appreciated and safe, her powerful ego and personality defenses slowly started melting away. As a result, for the first time in her life, Phyllis was able to get emotionally close to people and to allow people to get close to her. Phyllis and I have now become close friends and the static has disappeared.

The Persona

It is perfectly natural and normal for every young child to want to feel wanted, safe, loved, appreciated and accepted for who they really are. When a child doesn't get her basic needs met, either due to dysfunctional family dynamics, abuse or for other reasons, she might develop a persona that she hopes will be more acceptable to her parents than her authentic personality. Her persona can easily develop over time into a *mask* that the child uses to hide behind.

If the child doesn't feel safe being her authentic self, she might develop extremely dysfunctional coping or survival strategies, like protecting herself and getting negative attention by exploding, lashing out, or expressing resentment, anger or even rage. Or she might shut down, disappear, be extremely quiet and energetically leave her body, a pattern called *Disassociation*. These coping and survival patterns can create major mental, emotional, psychological and energetic challenges for the child, especially as she grows older.

Over time, some people begin to believe that they are their mask — they identify with the mask as themselves — even though it only builds a false identity. When this happens, tension builds between the authentic self, who wants to express itself and the false self, who is afraid to let go of control. These people have an unconscious fear that if the false self — the mask, the persona — is dropped, they might get hurt, disappointed, abandoned, rejected or in extreme situations, even killed.

This unconscious fear creates stress, tension and havoc in their lives. Unless this psychological and energetic disconnect is healed, the trapped and fearful energy will build and fester over time, increasing in intensity and will ultimately contaminate most if not all of the person's thoughts, attitudes, beliefs, interactions and relationships. It will also negatively impact and sabotage the person's health, well-being, personal relationships, finances and business interactions.

As psychological stress and tension build, a child may develop a nervous condition, experience anxiety or hypertension, become ill or in extreme cases, have a nervous breakdown. The conflict is clear: the authentic self, the soul and the healthy inner child are struggling to come out and be seen, while the scared child is petrified to let go of its persona and mask. The internal battle can be devastating.

Occasionally, people suddenly feel like they've had enough of feeling scared and living a lie, and they break free of their mask. When this happens they might suddenly, without warning, quit their job, give up their career, and even walk away from their marriage and children, in their quest to find their authentic self and do something different. Some call this a mid-life crisis. I call it a major mid-life breakthrough.

This life-altering experience happens when people finally feel they've had enough of hiding, playing safe, playing small, serving and pleasing everyone else. It's a time when they are finally ready and willing to begin to love, honor, respect and support themselves. They are ready to discover who they really are, what they really want out of life and what makes them happy. If they had shut down their aliveness at an early age, this sudden change may make them seem like a wild, irresponsible teenager. In reality, they are simply recovering their lost years. With time, they eventually settle down and integrate their breakthrough, and when they do, they become much more relaxed, authentic, happy, healthy, playful, creative and at peace with themselves.

Facing Ourselves

You might remember the first Star Wars movie, when Yoda, the wise Jedi master, instructed Luke Skywalker to descend into an underground cave where he must face a test and fight with another warrior. During the intense battle, Luke and his adversary seem equally matched. The shocker comes when Luke finally knocks the helmet off of his opponent, only to discover that he had been fighting himself.

This principle is a spiritual truth: our ultimate battle comes when we have to face ourselves — including our fears, insecurities, demons, limitations and negativity — so that we can break free from our old limiting beliefs and self-sabotaging patterns. It is the only way we can live a life that is true to ourselves, that is aligned with our truest values and that fulfills our soul purpose for living.

Joseph Campbell wrote about the myths, described in almost all cultures, which describe similar personal challenges that must be faced and achieved in order for the seeker or warrior to achieve his destiny. This journey is the quest for our personal Holy Grail.

Signs of a Dysfunctional Family

A long time ago, I learned there are three rules that dominate a dysfunctional family: Don't talk; don't trust; and don't feel. If we are to be functional and healthy, we must break these rules and learn to risk, trust, reach out, communicate, speak our truth and ask for help. We need to embrace and accept all of our feelings and emotions without judgment. Living a healthy life is not about looking good, being right or being in control. It is about staying energetically present, as well as being open, honest, vulnerable, authentic and in integrity with who we truly are.

A Psychological Perspective on Humans

Modern psychology has many different models to explain the way human beings think, behave and interact. The model most psychologists currently accept evaluates a human being from five very different perspectives. Each perspective interacts with and affects the others. These are not extreme black-or-white descriptions; everyone is a blend of several of these qualities and may be at one extreme in some areas while at the other extreme in other areas. People's behavior, actions and reactions can change depending upon the situation they are in, how safe and supported they feel, and how strongly they are committed to changing. No one can force anyone else to change and then expect that change to be real or to permanently take hold. A person has to want to change and be committed to changing.

EMOTIONAL STABILITY

People who are emotionally stable and mature rarely get wound up or up tight; they are easy-going, stay calm, present, centered and are thoughtful. When faced with challenges, they deal with them by communicating in a calm mature manner without becoming over-emotional or creating more drama. On the other hand, people who are negatively affected or emotionally unstable are reactive and are high maintenance. They can also be immature, shut down and withdrawn, unwilling or incapable of being emotionally present.

AFFECT

This aspect deals with how much positive emotion a person expresses. Most people with a positive affect are extroverts; they are smiling, happy, playful, outgoing and jovial. They easily lift the spirits and the energy of others when they enter a room or participate in a project. Low-affect people tend to be introverts who are quiet, withdrawn and depressed. They can pull down the positive energy of a group.

CONSCIENTIOUSNESS

Conscientious people have a strong internal sense of what needs to be done and they automatically take positive actions to complete these tasks. They are on time, dependable, aware of their surroundings, honest and can be trusted to do what they say they're going to do in the time frame they say they are going to do it. They have a strong value system, which makes them great friends, partners, employees and leaders. On the other hand, people who are not conscientious have a tendency to cut corners, skip tasks, be sloppy, messy and miss deadlines. They are generally irresponsible and usually do not make good friends, good employees, good leaders or good partners.

AGREEABLENESS

Agreeable people are easy to get along with; they are peacemakers, willing to talk openly and honestly to work things out. Even if they have a very different opinion than you do, they will still respect you and your opinion, and be able to get along with you. There have no need to limit, dominate, control you or convert you to their way of thinking and being. They are warm, responsible and easy to accept. Agreeable people do not react. On the other hand, disagreeable people love to fight, argue, disagree, scramble the energy, be sarcastic and bully others. They have a tendency to take the opposite position of any opinion, attitude or belief you have, just for fun. They are addicted to and thrive on negativity, conflict and chaos.

OPENNESS TO NEW EXPERIENCES

People who are open to new experiences are curious and intuitive. They find new things interesting, educational, exciting and energizing. They are open and receptive to learning, changing, growing and evolving. To them, life is a grand adventure to be fully lived. People who are not open to experience life and living fully have closed minds, are irritable, negative and resistant to anything new and different.

Ego/Personality (Negative) vs. Soul-Based (Positive) Values for Living Life

This table can be downloaded from my website at www.michaelbradford.com.

The Physical Body

When we are in spirit form, we are in a perfected state. We are immortal, all knowing and we are at one with ourselves and with the universe. We do not have to work, eat, think or be afraid. Survival is not an issue, as there are no bills to pay and no death. We are totally safe in Spirit.

Being on Earth, however, is an entirely different story! One requirement for coming to Earth and having an Earth experience is to have a physical body. And with your physical body comes senses that you will use to interact with life on the Earth plane. These include not only the physical senses — taste, touch, smell, hearing and sight — but also feelings, emotions and intuition. Depending on the lessons you have chosen for this lifetime, the body you chose to receive can be strong, healthy, whole and complete — or not. The lessons you chose before you incarnate determine the level of health you experience and how developed your senses will be.

When we incarnate into a physical body, we may experience challenges with thinking, feeling, emotions, courage, confidence, motivation, communication, eating, sleeping, health, exercise, physical strength, sexuality and much more.

The Body as an Energy System

Like all modern cities, the human body is made up of energy fields, networks and grids. For a city, these networks include roads, electrical lines, gas, water, sewer, telephone, Internet, cable TV, telephone towers, etc. The networks of the human body include the cardiovascular system, nervous system, endocrine system, muscles, bones, meridians and other systems. The overall energy system of the human body is called the Aura or the auric field.

The aura is a living bioelectric energy field that extends outwards from the physical body. This energy field is strongest and densest near the physical body, and then gets progressively weaker with distance away from the body. This is similar to the Earth's atmosphere, where the layers closest to the Earth are denser and then get progressively thinner the further away they become.

The strength, size and color of the human aura depends upon your personal energy levels, your health and your level of evolution. When your energy is low and depleted, the colors of your aura are muted, dull and weak and the auric field lies much closer to your body. When you are rested, happy, energized and feeling good, your energy level is higher and the auric field is brighter, stronger and extends out much further from your body. The higher your level of evolution, the brighter, stronger and larger your auric field will be.

Your aura is alive, constantly changing shape, size and colors depending upon what we are thinking, feeling and experiencing. Some people can see the actual colors of the aura, while others can only sense them. At the time of death, this energy field disappears.

Within the aura and aligned along the spine are seven major energy centers called *Chakras*. There are also meridians, which are energy and nerve lines running throughout the body, from head to toe. (Note: There are also many minor chakras.)

There are four major aspects to our human body experience: our mental body, consisting of our mind and thoughts; our physical body, consisting of blood vessels, nerves organs, bones, muscles and skin; our emotional body, made up of our feelings and emotions; and our spiritual body, consisting of the spiritual aspects of ourselves.

All of these parts interact like a giant mobile; where everything is interconnected and interdependent. When any one aspect moves or changes, it affects and changes our entire structure on all levels, throughout all dimensions.

The way I approach healing, coaching and consulting is by first intuitively scanning and reading a client's physical body, their energy field and their soul. Then I access the highest levels of consciousness possible, far above third-dimensional reality, to get the precise information the person needs at the time in order to heal, transform or to resolve their challenges. Healing that is done on higher levels of consciousness ensures that the information received is extremely accurate. It also ensures that the results are almost instantaneous and are more complete. Another benefit is that healing done at higher dimensions minimizes the pain and trauma often associated with normal healing done solely on the third-dimensional level.

* * *

John, a businessman in his late 60s, was involved in a serious car accident. His car was stopped at a traffic light when he was hit so hard from behind that both cars were totaled. John was severely shaken. Although he went to the hospital and had X-rays, an EEG, CAT scan and an MRI, there were no indications of any broken bones, internal injuries or anything out of the ordinary. The medical doctors could not find anything "medically" wrong with John.

John experienced what the medical profession is now calling Post Concussion Syndrome and he went through 16 months of intense stiffness, pain and suffering. As time progressed, the symptoms seemed to change location and move around his body. The main physical areas affected were his upper and lower back, shoulders and right foot. He had sharp pains behind his eyes, pain in his ears, as well as other bodily aches and pains. His vision changed and he also experienced headaches, tiredness, exhaustion, lack of concentration, sleep challenges, memory challenges, fogginess, confusion and disorientation. Although John had been a workaholic prior to the accident, after the accident, he could accomplish very little except to rest and allow his body to heal, readjust, recalibrate and integrate the new energy.

One psychologist told John that his car accident was similar to a lightning bolt hitting a building: after a lightning strike, all the clocks, TV, internet and other electrical devices have to be reset. John needed his entire system reset.

This resetting process is necessary whenever a person experiences a severe accident, loss, shock or trauma. The human body's autonomic nervous system (its fight or flight programming), the right and left-brain integration, the mind-body-spirit connection and the individual's spiritual connection all have to be reset and come into alignment.

After any severe shock, trauma or loss, the body has to mentally, physically, emotionally and spiritually heal, to re-align, recalibrate and re-integrate itself. It is not unusual for a person experiencing this resetting process to change either in a positive way — by becoming more sensitive, caring, loving, compassionate and creative — or in a negative way, by shutting down and becoming more angry and bitter.

It is important to be aware that time alone does not usually completely heal a person who has experienced a significant shock, loss, trauma, surgery or accident. This is especially true for children. In these and in many other cases, completing the healing process requires the clearing, re-adjustment, re-alignment and re-balancing of the person's aura and energy field for maximum healing and reintegration to be achieved. It is also important to identify, clear and release any fears or negative thought patterns regarding life and living, and to replace these with positive uplifting life-affirming ones.

Although this healing process can sometimes appear to be very subtle, the results can be life-changing and can often be accomplished in one session.

* * *

Jane, an American woman in her late 50s, had surgery on her foot. For many years afterwards, she experienced pain in the area where the surgery had been done. No matter what the doctor's did, which included re-operating on her foot, the pain would not go away. The doctors were baffled and could not offer any explanation or solution.

When I met Jane, she shared this information with me and asked for my help. Gently I assisted her to clear her aura and especially her energy field in the vicinity of the surgery on her foot. I also cleared and rebalanced the energy around her heart, which was still holding some of the trauma from the accident and the surgery. As I was assisting her, she described feeling as if I was gently taking a sock off of her foot. By the end of this process, which lasted less than 15 minutes, the pain was totally gone and she has been pain free ever since.

Whenever you experience an accident, surgery, shock, trauma, loss or even a setback, your aura, your energy field, and your physical body are affected. This is why it is so important for you to have your energy field cleared, re-adjusted, re-aligned and re-balanced, so that your full healing and reintegration can be achieved.

This clearing and healing process can be achieved equally well either in-person, by phone or via Skype video conferencing.

* * *

During a corporate presentation, Paula, a highly qualified woman in her early 30's, asked for my help. She explained that she wanted to be a full-time trainer, however she was so oversensitive and so overwhelmed by people's energy that this was undermining her ability to be effective at her job.

When I checked her aura, her energy field, I discovered that it extended out far beyond that of most people. In fact, her energy field extended out further than any other person's energy field I had ever measured under normal conditions.

The auric field of a healthy person will normally extend out only about 6 to 36 inches from the physical body. When I checked Paula's energy field, it extended out well beyond 20 feet, over 240 inches.

This told me that Paula's aura was far too energetically open and, hence she was vulnerable to being affected by all energies within a 20 feet radius of her. Picking up and being triggered by all of these energies would scramble anyone's energy field. No wonder she was having a challenge with staying focused and being energetically clear.

The first thing I did was to teach Paula how to sense her own energy. Then I taught her how to pull her energy field in closer to her physical body, so that she would not be picking up all the discordant energy and energetic static around her. Next I taught her how to pull her energy field completely into her physical body, and finally I had her imagine zipping herself and her energy field up in a Lycra bodysuit, like the movie character Catwoman. This fully contained and shielded her energy.

As she did this, Paula instantly felt a positive shift as her energy levels strengthened. She described herself as feeling less scrambled, much stronger, clearer, more alive and vibrant, and more grounded. Everyone in the room watching her could see a tangible increase in her positive energy. She stood taller, radiating courage and confidence.

With this new awareness, Paula was confident that she could now follow her heart and become the trainer she always wanted to be. This entire process took only about 20 minutes.

Chapter 7
The Human Mind

The Mind

Our minds are active every second of every day — even when we are asleep. In ancient times, people's minds and senses protected them, kept them alive, and helped them to find food and shelter. In current times, now that our basic survival needs are met, our minds are busy with thinking, planning, analyzing, organizing and controlling. Because our thoughts are so critical to our survival, happiness and success, it is important to understand how the mind works.

We can let our minds be undisciplined and take the risk that they might work against us, or we can discipline and train our minds to serve us in a healthy way. The three basic aspects to the mind — the conscious mind, the subconscious mind and the super conscious mind — each have a unique function that serves us in a particular way.

The Conscious Mind

The mind can be compared to an iceberg. Just as only 10% of an iceberg is visible above the surface of the water, only 10% of our mind is conscious. And as the other 90% of an iceberg is invisible and hidden below the surface, you could say the same of our subconscious mind. Our conscious mind is only the very tip of the visible iceberg, compared to the vastness of the subconscious mind hidden below the surface.

The conscious mind has two hemispheres. The left-brain — considered the more masculine energy side — is designed to observe, think, analyze, calculate and reason. It wants to understand, quantify, figure things out and make meaning out of everything. The right brain — considered the more feminine energy side — Is designed to sense and feel. It is more creative, emotional and intuitive. Most men tend to be more left brain, logically dominant, whereas most women tend to be more right brain, feeling, sensing, intuitive and emotionally dominant.

The conscious mind is constantly sifting through the information presented to it and making decisions designed to protect us, keep us safe and ensure our survival. As long the conscious mind is positively programmed, getting accurate information and functioning well, it can be of great service to us.

However, if the conscious mind is not functioning well or the information presented to the conscious mind is contaminated and distorted by unfounded fears, negative thoughts, attitudes, limiting beliefs and unresolved issues, then the decisions it makes will be inaccurate and less than optimum. It will fail to protect us, and it will endanger the quality of our lives. Distorted decisions can sabotage and undermine all of our positive efforts, including our joy, happiness, relationships, success, prosperity, finances and business opportunities. No matter how hard we work, we can seldom identify and overcome these distortions and blockages on our own without skilled professional assistance.

This is why it is so critical to do our deep inner healing and energy clearing so that these negative programs, contaminants, distortions and self-sabotage patterns are eliminated. The clearer we are, the more effectively the conscious mind can function and the easier it is to create joy, happiness, healthy relationships, success, prosperity and profitable business opportunities.

* * *

Bill, an American man in his late 40s, had difficulty accepting help and support from others, and letting people get close to him. He believed he had to remain in control and do everything by himself. Growing up in an environment where his father was unstable, Bill learned that people's loyalty and affections can change quickly. As an adult, Bill still carried his unresolved childhood pain; he found it very hard to trust anyone or to let anyone get close to him. Even if people were kind and caring, Bill felt uneasy and would either want to push the person away or to run away. Even when there was no actual current threat to Bill, his unresolved history haunted him, undermining and sabotaging his ability to trust, and to accept love, support and success.

The negative programming and energetic imprint that remained in Bill's conscious and subconscious memory had to be released before he could ever hope to achieve any long-term meaningful connection with people and achieve success.

Unfortunately, in an attempt to keep him safe and protect him from getting hurt again, Bill's conscious mind was sabotaging him and keeping him from relaxing, trusting and allowing good, kind people to support him. It was also keeping him from attracting a loving partner.

* * *

George was a New Zealand man in his late 40s who invited me to his home to meet his wife and children. Over the next few months, we became very good friends. One day, as his two young children were playing, I suggested that we both get down on all fours, like horses and let his kids ride on our backs. My father had done this with me as a child and it was a fun game. Once I made the suggestion, George's attitude towards me changed dramatically. After that, our relationship became strained and our friendship abruptly ended. I was confused and disappointed.

Months later, I learned that when George was a child, his cousins had sexually abused him while they were playing. To protect his children, he remained both emotionally and physically distant from them, and would not interact much, hug or even play with his children. George's conscious mind and subconscious mind were attempting to protect him from his painful memories, and to protect his children from possibly being hurt and abused. George did not want to pass on the abuse that happened to him.

A much healthier way that George could have dealt with his painful memories would have been for him to seek help for healing his issues. If he had, it would have eliminated his pain and suffering. It would have also stopped him from sabotaging his healthy relationship with his children and from negatively affecting their development. Unfortunately, by emotionally shutting down and distancing himself from his children, George passed on his pain, suffering and dysfunctional behavior to his children. Unresolved challenges like these can be passed down through a family lineage and lead to many generations of anger, hurt, pain, guilt, shame, suffering and dysfunctional behavior.

The Subconscious Mind

The subconscious, also referred to as the Unconscious mind, is like a computer hard drive or a memory storage device. Stored within it are all of our memories, thoughts, attitudes, beliefs and programming. It also contains vivid full-color moving pictures of all our experiences, including all smells, tastes and sounds. Using intuitive energy tracking, deep relaxation and guided meditation techniques, we can recall memories from our past, including other lifetimes.

It is important to note that the subconscious mind does not assign any emotions or meaning to our memories, nor does it judge them. The subconscious mind is simply the record holder. Assigning meaning, making judgments and feeling emotions is strictly the job of the conscious mind.

The subconscious mind does not think or reason. When fully accessed, it accepts all suggestions and instructions, and follows all directions without questioning whether or not the activity is logical, wise, appropriate or even possible. On the other hand, it is the job of the conscious mind to protect, filter and prevent access to the subconscious mind. A person who is deeply relaxed or in a trance, even a light trance, can achieve almost superhuman feats when the filtering of the conscious mind has been suspended.

I've personally experienced walking on hot coals without being burnt (it felt like walking on popcorn), bending 3/8" rebar steel with my throat, picking up heavy weights, speeding up and slowing down time, and many other seemingly impossible experiences — and have taught others to do the same. This is why learning how to access and direct the subconscious mind can be so powerful.

What's challenging is that the conscious mind guards and protects access to the subconscious mind; so it is not very easy to reach into it and program it the way we would want it. Fortunately, I have been trained by human teachers, my spiritual guides and teachers, and by my intuition to track, sense, monitor, access and positively reprogram both the conscious and subconscious mind.

By accessing subconscious memories from this and past lives, we can often get precise information that can dramatically improve our health, relationships, finances and success. Almost all challenges are caused either by subconscious negative thoughts, attitudes and beliefs or by unresolved losses, shocks and traumas. A highly skilled intuitive can quickly and easily access, identify and clear these blockages.

* * *

After being introduced to hypnosis in 1972 and Neuro-Linguistic-Programming (NLP) in 1981, I earned my Master and Trainer certifications. Over the decades since then, I have developed my own unique ways to quickly access and reprogram both the conscious and the unconscious mind. My unique approach greatly accelerates a client's learning and healing process. Neuro-Linguistic-Programming, hypnosis and self-hypnosis are good; however using my intuition to read energy patterns is faster, more precise and reaches a lot deeper. While assisting clients, I maintain a high frequency energy field. This allows me to link with, energetically access, communicate with and help to positively reprogram a client's conscious, subconscious and super-conscious mind.

One of my dreams is to teach the advanced techniques I have developed to others, especially those who have already been trained in Neuro-Linguistic-Programming, hypnosis, self-hypnosis, Reiki and other forms of energy healing.

* * *

In 1972, I worked and trained with a world-class hypnotist. At one of his events, he invited me to participate in a demonstration. There were about a dozen people in the room. I was asked to stand up straight and keep my eyes closed. Then, using his voice, he deeply relaxed me and guided me into a light trance. He kept telling me that my body was turning into a bar of steel — a rigid bar of steel. He kept repeating the suggestion as he firmly patted my arms, back and legs.

After a few minutes, four people from the group picked me up by my arms and legs. They then placed me horizontally face up, with the back of my head resting on one chair and the heels of my shoes on another chair, and with nothing underneath me. With my eyes still shut, they repeated the suggestion to me over and over again. Suddenly, I felt a light pressure on my thighs. I waited about five seconds and then being curious, I opened my eyes to see what was going on. I was shocked to see a woman, who weighed about 135 pounds, standing on top of me with one foot on each of my thighs. Totally surprised, I collapsed and fell to the floor. Had I not opened my eyes, I could have very easily continued to support the woman who was standing on top of me.

That is how amazing the subconscious mind can be. It is also the reason why this powerful tool has to be used ethically, respectfully and appropriately.

* * *

We've all heard of stories about a mother who lifted a car or other heavy object off of a child who was pinned underneath. Those are examples of someone who, without even thinking, accessed the power of their subconscious and super-conscious minds, and performed what some people would call a miracle. You can call it a miracle or you can be more accurate by saying that the person went into an altered state, accessed their subconscious and super-conscious minds, and did what they knew needed to be done to save the child.

* * *

The subconscious mind is so powerful that it can greatly influence our physical bodies. There is a story of a man who was found dead in a refrigerated railway car. All of his bodily symptoms were exactly the same as if he had died from freezing. But those investigating the case were baffled: the refrigerated railway car had been taken out of service because its cooling unit was broken. It could not have reduced the temperature enough to freeze anything. In fact, the actual temperature in the railway car was well above the freezing mark. Yet the man had convinced himself that he was freezing to death, so his unconscious mind obliged him and created the reality he expected.

Note: We always create the reality we are consciously and unconsciously expecting!

The Super-conscious Mind

The super-conscious mind is connected to Universal Consciousness. It operates like an energetic internet, with instant total access to all of the information in the universe from the beginning of time until the end of time. It has no limits or boundaries. Anything and everything you desire to know is instantly available. Everyone has unlimited access to this resource and, with training and experience, it becomes easier and easier to instantly access the information it holds.

When I work with a client, I first set my intention to assist them and ask to be of Divine service. Then I use my intuition to ask my super-conscious mind to access the precise information that will allow me to best serve my client. In fact, whenever I write, speak to a group, coach, mentor, do a healing session or teach a workshop, I raise my soul frequency and vibration as high as possible, enter into an altered state, and connect with my higher consciousness and my super-conscious mind.

Another way of explaining this is to say that I energetically merge with the Knowing Field, the Morphogenetic Field, the super-conscious field to gain access to the precise information that my client is seeking. Accessing this field provides profound life-changing insights, guidance, answers and solutions.

Negative and Positive Mindset

Our mindsets, the ways we think about and approach life, can change depending upon how confident we are with what we are doing, our history, our environment and the way we are feeling in the moment. Few people are totally confident in all areas of their life. We all experience a wide range of feelings, emotions and sometimes think very positively, while at other times we hesitate, doubt and question ourselves. This is normal and to be expected; however people tend to have either a more positive or a more negative mindset.

People with an extremely negative mindset consider themselves to be powerless victims who have little or no control over their actions, their life, their fate or their destiny. They are like a rudderless ship, blown every which way by the wind and by life. Many people with a negative mindset suffer from low self-image and self-esteem. They tend to be Super Pleasers, waiting for someone outside of themselves to take control of their life and to tell them what to think, what to believe, how to act and what to do. Often these people are waiting for someone else to take responsibility for them, to rescue them and to fix their life. They tend to be confused, lazy, depressed and take few positive actions to support or improve themselves, or the conditions of their life.

People with negative, self-defeating mindsets usually say things such as "I can't," "It will never work," "Why bother," "It won't matter anyway," "I don't know," "It's useless to try," "No matter how hard I try, it won't work out anyway," "I'm doing the best I can," "It's hopeless," and "It will take a long time." They come up with hundreds of excuses for why they cannot achieve their goals. Unfortunately, when you try to help a victim, even though they cry out, begging you for help and support, they will frequently argue, fight, resist, negate and discount any assistance you offer them.

On the other hand, people who have a positive mindset are usually more confident, more willing to take full responsibility for themselves and more proactive in their lives. When faced with a challenge or an opportunity, they take positive steps towards achieving their goals. They are more comfortable and confident doing research, talking to people, asking questions, asking for help and allowing people to help them. Once positive people put their minds to something, they usually achieve it. Although challenges still come up, they will do their absolute best to find positive ways to solve those challenges.

People with a positive mindset are usually curious, resourceful, inquisitive and will not take *No* for an answer. They look for ways to improve themselves and to achieve their goals. If one pathway is blocked, they will seek other avenues. They think outside of the box and are willing to ask the hard questions that many other people may think to be too personal, unkind, silly, strange or ridiculous.

Positive mindset people love to be challenged, receive suggestions, get feedback and work as part of a co-creative team. People who are around them feel uplifted, energized and inspired.

To create a positive mindset for yourself, be mindful of where you focus your attention, how you manage your emotions and the words you use when you speak. When people are operating out of lack, fear and insecurity, they usually have a negative mindset. When a person is more comfortable and at peace with themselves, they tend to be more confident and have a more positive mindset.

As you are willing to learn, change, grow and be supported in clearing your limiting beliefs, self-sabotage patterns and unconscious blockages, you automatically develop a more positive mindset. When this happens, you become healthier, happier, more peaceful, attract higher quality relationships and achieve greater success — all with much less effort. Long term coaching ensures your continued positive progress and is especially helpful for professionals and entrepreneurs.

Chapter 8
Learning Lessons

Learning Curves

A learning curve — the rate at which a person learns — is determined by two variables. The first is the amount and intensity of the learning, and the second is the speed at which a person is willing to learn his lessons. Some people like to do one thing at a time, go slowly and take their time. For them, the learning curve may not be very steep or challenging. At the other end of the spectrum, some people may want to learn a lot in a short amount of time, even in one lifetime, and hence may choose very challenging situations to gain experience quickly.

For example, a person who wants to take her time to get through a four-year college may take five to six years to do so. However, a person who is very impatient and driven may complete her schooling at the same college in three years or less.

Applying this principle to the study of mathematics, one person may be satisfied by simply learning addition and subtraction in this lifetime. Another person may want to learn addition and subtraction, plus multiplication and division. A third person may want to learn all of those, plus algebra, geometry, trigonometry and calculus.

Prior to coming to Earth, we choose the main subjects we wish to focus on and the speed at which we wish to learn these lessons. Our free will allows us to choose whether we fulfill our soul agreements or not. It is entirely up to us.

Speedboats and Oil Tankers

Each of us learns, changes and grows at our own unique speed. Some people are fast and agile learners and integrate new information quickly. Other people take time to digest and integrate new information, and so they may change more slowly. Neither approach is good nor bad; they are just two different ways of processing and integrating information.

Some people are like agile speedboats, which can change direction almost instantly and can respond to any situation very quickly. Other people are more like huge lumbering oil tankers, which move very slowly. The only way you can tell if an oil tanker has changed direction is to look behind it and to see whether the wake in back of the boat is straight or curved.

It is not unusual for people to cover both ends of the spectrum: acting like a speedboat in one situation and more like an oil tanker in others. Please note that speed alone doesn't get you brownie points; we humans don't get extra credit for learning things quickly, only for learning and integrating lessons.

The Purpose of Challenges

Most of us would like to live a loving, quiet, peaceful and abundant life, and to assist others to do the same. However life is filled with challenges. As we develop spiritually, we learn that our tests and challenges are often great gifts in disguise. It is natural and normal, from our limited human perspective, to want to feel safe, be loved and get all of our needs met. From a spiritual perspective however, we purposely attract people and challenges to trigger us, shake us up and speed up our learning, changing and growing process.

What is interesting is that our greatest growth lessons often come from the tests and trials we experience, and the mistakes we make. These challenges stretch us and motivate us to discover new creative ways to solve problems and achieve our goals. When we get things right the first time, we do not necessarily learn a lot. Only when we have to challenge ourselves and expand our consciousness do we really learn, change and grow.

Helping versus Crippling

There are many times when we sincerely want to help others, especially children and people in crisis. The challenge is, if we are not conscious and careful in the way we approach helping others, we can unintentionally end up doing more harm than good. Although our intentions may be good, we can even end up crippling a person, rather than helping them.

There is a religious saying that states, "If you give a person a fish, you feed them for the day. However, if you teach them how to fish, you feed them for a lifetime." Over the years, I've attempted to help friends and colleagues in many ways. I have loaned them money and even brought them into my own home. In most cases, I ended up losing my money, my privacy and my friends. I learned the hard way that the best way to help people is to compassionately listen to them, give them honest feedback, coach them, offer them intuitive healing and guidance, and then allow them to choose for themselves whether to take the actions needed or not. I have learned that, in most cases, people need to take full responsibility for straightening out their own lives.

In extreme situations, like dealing with drug addicts and alcoholics, it is easy to get sucked into their victim mentality and the trauma-drama of their situation. Although some drug addicts and alcoholics can be helped, many have to first bottom out — to reach a really low point — even facing death, before they are open, receptive and willing to take responsibility for themselves and changing their lives.

A butterfly is a perfect example of this principle. When a butterfly starts to come out of the larvae, it struggles. This struggling helps the newborn butterfly to pump blood into its wings, which in turn fully extends and strengthens their wings. This also allows the wings to dry. If we, in our desire to be helpful, assist in pulling the butterfly out of its cocoon, the wings will never fully develop and extend. Our attempt to help the butterfly will cripple it for life and cause it to die. Sometimes being too helpful is actually hurtful.

Understanding Anchoring

Anchoring is a form of conditioning that happens when repetition of a sound, thought, feeling or action is planted into a person's or animal's neurological system and consciousness. The best example of this is the scientific experiment when the physiologist, Ivan Pavlov, rang a bell every time he fed some dogs. Within a very short time, the dogs would salivate any time they heard the bell ring. The results of this conditioning can be positive or negative, depending upon the way it is used. This is the reason why it is very important to understand what anchoring is, and the effect it has upon motivation and development.

If a child comes home from school complaining she had a bad day, her parent might say, "Come here, I'll fix you something to eat and you will feel better." If this happens three times, the child could very easily develop an eating disorder or a weight issue that she will suffer from for the rest of her life. It only takes three times for a conditioning to become anchored into someone's neurological system, as well as into their conscious and subconscious minds. This is especially true when the words or actions originate from a trusted authority figure.

By giving the child food, rather than assisting them to face and deal with the emotional upset, the parent is unknowingly programming the child to ignore her emotions, and to swallow and stuff her upset along with the food. The food, love, attention, comfort and support get linked together. In this situation, it would've been much healthier if the parent had sat down with the child and asked her to tell them what happened, what she learned and what she could have possibly done differently. This approach would have taught the child healthy communication skills and emotional maturity. (Note: When a parent offers the child food instead of talking issues through, it is usually because the parent is uncomfortable and unskilled in talking about and dealing with his or her own feelings and emotions.)

If a child falls off his bicycle and gets hurt and a parent runs over and gives him unconditional love, there is a chance that the child will associate accidents with getting unconditional love. If this association is made, then every time he wants unconditional love, he may unconsciously create accidents to get attention. The best way to handle this, unless it is a medical emergency, is to wait until the child stops crying and then talk to him, asking him what he learned from the situation and what he would do differently next time. Again, this teaches the child that mistakes, accidents and failures are simply a normal part of life. It also teaches the child how to verbalize his feelings and emotions, and supports him in learning how to take care of himself.

Manifestation and Creation

The process of creation and manifestation on Earth is very different than it is in Spirit, on other planets and in other dimensions. The three-dimensional Earth frequency and vibration is much slower, lower and denser, hence it takes much more time, energy, effort, clarity and focus to create on the Earth plane. This is the main reason people get so frustrated and disheartened when attempting to create on Earth.

Most of us come from planets and dimensions where we just have to think a thought, and whatever we are thinking instantly manifests in the precise way we wish it to manifest. There is no need to work hard, nor is there any time delay for our desires to manifest: it is instantaneously manifested. The challenges and frustrations we experience here on Earth with the manifestation process are part of our testing and learning. As a human, we have to learn to be more patient, and to learn to focus our thoughts, feelings, emotions, mental pictures and energy more effectively. We also have to learn to remain focused over longer periods of time and to maintain a very positive mental attitude.

On Earth it takes at least ten times more focus, energy and time to manifest our desires and creations. Since the process requires so much more energy, plus a tremendous amount of patience, many people get frustrated when it appears that no matter how hard they pray, visualize or put energy into manifesting their project, their dreams will never come true.

There is, however, something we can do something about it. The clearer our thoughts, feelings, emotions, visualizations, intentions and our energy are, the faster and easier we are able to manifest our desires. If fear, insecurity, low self-image, low self-esteem, negative programming, unresolved issues or energy blockages plague us, the energy will be scrambled and our ability to manifest will be greatly reduced. There are also other factors negatively affecting our ability to manifest, including karma, past life vows and other unconscious patterns.

Most, if not all, of these blockages can be pinpointed and released fairly quickly and easily, often in a single session, with the assistance of a highly-skilled professional intuitive coach who can accurately track and clear energy blockages.

Over the years, I have given talks to Law of Attraction groups and during the demonstrations assisted participants to identify what was sabotaging their manifestation process. In most cases, the main blockages could be identified and released fairly easily, often in a matter of minutes.

Soulmates

A lot has been written about soulmates. In this lifetime, I have met many of my soulmates from other times and places. I believe that, unless there is a specific soul agreement made before incarnating this lifetime, we can choose to be with any one of a number of potential partners — hence, it is up to us to choose wisely.

Sometimes we meet people from other countries and cultures whose beliefs and values are very different from our own. There are even times when we do not speak the same language and, yet, the chemistry, overwhelming magnetic attraction and familiarity between us are tangible, powerful, unmistakable and unavoidable.

To assist us in our soul growth, our soul, as well as our guides and teachers, attract to us the perfect lessons, experiences and people we need to interact with so that we can learn, change and grow. We will also be guided to experiences and trials that will challenge us and assist us to mentally, physically, emotionally and spiritually progress. Either we learn from our lessons and keep moving forward, or we will continue to attract and experience the same type of lessons, over and over, until we finally choose to face and to learn our lessons. If, when and how we do this is always our choice!

Soul Magnets

Our souls operate like a giant magnet, attracting to us the perfect people, places, situations and opportunities that will allow us to both challenge and support ourselves. Our souls long to learn, change, risk and grow. We only attract the people and situations that have the perfect lessons to teach us, or the perfect gifts to give us! We are seldom attracted to people if there are no lessons to be learned. In business, friendships and romantic relationships, most of us are only attracted to people who are on the same frequency as we are and who we have something in common or resonate with.

Depending on our soul lessons, we may also have times — even lifetimes — that our lessons are more focused on resting, relaxing, recovering and integrating. Remember, we are never given more than we can handle — and we are the ones who set all of this up in the first place. Remember that there are no victims on planet Earth!

Guides and Teachers

This section may well raise a few eyebrows and stir up some intense feelings and emotions. However, I write this from first-hand, personal experience and I absolutely do not intend any disrespect towards guides, teachers or beings of light!

We attract guides and teachers to us for a number of reasons. One reason is for them to help us from the spiritual dimension and another is to offer them the opportunity to learn from us what it is like to experience the Earth plane. It is a two-way, joint-learning experience! Some of these guides and teachers have had prior Earth lifetime experiences, while others have not had any human incarnations.

Depending upon their level of evolution, skills, expertise and learning experiences, our guides and teachers might or might not be more knowledgeable and qualified than we are.

If they have not had many — or any — Earth lifetime experiences, they will not fully understand nor appreciate the level of anxiety, fear, frustration or intense emotions that we experience as humans. It's important to understand that guides and teachers are not all-knowing, all-seeing and totally wise beings! They are on their paths of learning just as we are and they might or might not be that wise or that far ahead of us! Remember, they do not have to pay the earthly consequences we do, like feeling the emotional pain or experiencing loss, if they make a mistake. We alone suffer the consequences of our decisions and actions.

* * *

Many years ago I was in a relationship where my partner, Sandra and I would sometimes undergo intense learning experiences that some would call "conflicts." One day, in the middle of an intense argument, my partner looked at me and said, "What are we fighting about? I do not want to fight with you! Something else is going on here. Please help me. Please guide me into a very relaxed state, so I can go deep inside myself and scan my energy field to see what is going on!" (Note: To surrender like this in the middle of intense emotions takes tremendous faith, trust, courage and maturity. This is especially true if the person assisting you is the same person as the one who triggered you!)

As I guided Sandra deep into her own inner-knowing, she was able to clearly see that she had a guide who was an old nun. This guide did not want Sandra to be in a relationship with a man. I also discovered that I had an old male religious guide who was frugal and fearful about money matters.

When my partner came back to conscious awareness, we aligned our energies and said some prayers, demanding that all guides and teachers who were not in support of our relationship to be blessed and be gone! This created more positive energy in the relationship for a while. Unfortunately, we had other issues and the relationship later ended.

* * *

There are some interesting things to remember about guides and teachers. You can attract, hire and fire them, just as you can with advisors, coaches, employees and workers on the Earth plane. You can also outgrow your guides and teachers.

You can hold onto them, consciously or unconsciously, out of a sense of friendship, complacency, duty, loyalty, past life vows, tradition, fear or laziness. The challenge is that holding on to them for longer than is appropriate does not help you or them! When it is time to move on, thank and bless these guides and teachers for their service and let them — and yourself — move forward.

My intuition tells me that a full 80% of the human population is holding on to at least one guide that they have outgrown and no longer serves them. I've developed a special ceremony I use to assist my clients and workshop attendees to update their guides and teachers. Please email if you would like more information regarding this.

Programming and Re-programming

From the time we are in the womb until the time we leave our parental home, most of us are constantly being taught, educated and programmed with regards to what to think, what to feel and the right way to do things. During this time, we are taught values, interaction patterns, boundaries and other life skills. Our challenge in life is to keep making life-affirming positive choices and changes. We do this by constantly learning, changing, growing, upgrading and re-inventing ourselves.

Today, many children, even pre-teens, are much more skilled at using computers and technology than adults. Although it is very easy to see how keeping up with the latest technology is important in our lives, many of us fail to realize how important it is to keep up with changes and advances in personal and interpersonal skills, such as personal communication, interaction patterns, intimacy, connection, love, support, health and wellbeing.

If we want to stay mentally, emotionally, energetically and spiritually current, we must continually reevaluate and upgrade our thoughts, attitudes, beliefs, thinking processes, energy and intuition.

Especially when considering the rapid pace of change in today's world, we cannot afford to allow ourselves to become stagnant or complacent. Keeping our minds and energy fields clear and strong will greatly facilitate and support this process!

Free Will

Earth is one of the few places of learning in the universe where we have and can use our free will. Our ultimate test is how we use it. Do we use our free will from the soul level to help and support the "Highest Good of All Concerned" or do we use it from the ego and personality level for our own selfish gratification purposes?

A delicate balance exists between what we commit to achieve and learn here on Earth, and how we choose to use our free will. Our free will is our "wild card" and we can play it at any time we wish. Should we use it inappropriately, we may have to pay the price and suffer the consequences, especially if we go against the soul commitments we made prior to incarnating this lifetime.

* * *

There have been many times in my life when I had to make very challenging decisions with little or no guidance, or support from other humans. Deciding whether to continue to stay in high school and college or to drop out was a major life-changing choice for me. After graduating high school, I was living on my own and had no financial or emotional support from my father. Not only did I persevere and finish college by attending classes during the days, nights and summers, while working a full time job, I also went back years later and earned a Masters Degree in International Management.

One of the scariest decisions I ever made was to walk away from a very secure job I had as president of a manufacturing company. It was 1979 and I was 35 years old. I was single, living in Dallas, Texas, making an excellent salary plus bonus, had a company car, a four-bedroom house that I lived in alone, a rental property and stocks. I was also Vice President of a very large singles group. On the surface, I had it all. Yet something deep inside of me was beckoning me to walk away from everything and to start traveling. So I did. As someone who did not have much financial or emotional support while growing up, this decision was huge for me! However my inner prompting was so strong that I could not ignore it.

Another challenging decision I made was to travel by myself for six months leaving from the United Kingdom to Nepal, Thailand, Malaysia, Hong Kong, Singapore, Australia and New Zealand when I was very low on money and had only my credit card. It required supreme faith and tremendous trust. The universe stepped in and helped me: a complete stranger — a woman from Australia who used to be a travel agent — called me. I have no idea how she got my contact details, however she gave me several suggestions that provided me with the additional courage and confidence I needed at that time to take the trip. Luckily, the trip was a huge success.

$$* * *$$

Many years ago, I was told about a lifetime that I lived on another planet where I was being trained to be the capstone of a very special energy pyramid. According to the reading, I had special talents and was the only one in the group who was skilled enough to fill the capstone position. The group was relying on me to do this part. The reading said that I met another energy being, became enamored and wanted to travel around the universe with this energy being. Since I was pulled between my attraction to the energy and my commitment to the group, I met with the group to discuss it. The group said that the decision was entirely my choice: I had free will. However, without my presence and my unique skills, the project would have to be abandoned. I chose to travel with the energy for some time and then we separated, going our own ways. In my understanding, there was no karmic debt in this interaction — only free will and choice. My sense of it now is that the pyramid group will come back together in the near future to complete this project from a higher level of consciousness.

(Note: There are times when we do not incur a karmic debt or additional consequences for our actions and choices, however there are other times when we have committed on a soul level to do something and, if we abandon it, we can create a karmic debt to others or to ourselves. Along with our choices, usually come consequences.)

Is Life a Battlefield or a Playground?

There are many ways to approach our Earth adventure. One way is to live life as if we are playing in a giant playground where we are safe to explore and enjoy everything. In this scenario, we will probably approach life with our heart open, and remain trusting and curious about everyone and everything. The other extreme is to believe and behave as if life is a battlefield where we cannot trust anyone, and must constantly protect and defend ourselves from others. In this scenario, we may withdraw and shut down, or believe that we have to dominate and control others in order to survive and be safe.

* * *

There's a story about a clinical study in which two 9-year-old boys were brought in. One child was an optimist while the other was a pessimist. They put the optimist in a room filled with horse manure piled 3 feet high and they put the pessimist in a room filled with new toys and stuffed animals. After leaving the children alone for about 30 minutes, the psychologists returned to check on them. When they walked down the hallway towards the room where the optimist was, they could hear him shouting, "Yippee" and "Wahoo." When they opened the door, they found the optimist digging deep into the horse manure, throwing it in the air and smiling. When the psychologists asked the optimist why he was so happy, the child said, "With all this horse manure, there has to be a pony in here somewhere!"

When the psychologists approached the room with the pessimistic child, all they could hear was silence. When they opened the door, they found him sitting in the corner. When they asked why he was sitting in the corner, he said, "I'm afraid of breaking something." Whether it's true or not, this story is a good example of how a person's thoughts, attitudes and beliefs can greatly affect the way they approach and interact with life.

The Law of Attraction and
The Law of Manifestation

Like the law of gravity, the laws of the universe always work perfectly. When we focus on, look for and see the best in people and situations, we usually get what we consciously and unconsciously believe and expect.

When we go into a situation angry, tense, guarded and defensive, our fear and negative emotions will normally trigger a negative reaction in the people we are interacting with. When we are calm, trusting and have a positive mental attitude, we are more likely to create peace, harmony and co-creation with others. It has been proven that we attract experiences that reflect what we are consciously and unconsciously thinking and feeling.

Many people were very drawn to the book entitled "The Secret," which talks about the Law of Attraction and the Law of Manifestation. These Universal Laws always work perfectly all of the time. However, when we are not able to create and attract the love, happiness, prosperity, relationship, success or other things we are wanting in our lives, the problem is not with these Laws. The challenge is with our conscious and unconscious negative thoughts, attitudes and beliefs.

When our mental, physical, emotional and spiritual energies are positive, crystal clear and perfectly aligned, we can quickly and easily create our hearts desire. However when our thoughts, attitudes and beliefs are contaminated by unresolved conscious and unconscious fears, hurts, anger, shocks and traumas, this scrambles the energy, therefore undermining, sabotaging and blocking us from creating our hearts desires.

Tracking the energy to pinpoint exactly what is undermining, blocking and stopping a person from creating the life of their dreams is one of my specialties. When the source of this blocked energy is cleared and properly aligned, you are better able to attract what you desire in life — and you are able to do this faster, more easily, more completely and more often.

* * *

Many years ago, I was invited to speak to a large Law of Attraction group in the Middle East. After giving my talk and explaining who I am and what I have learned, I asked for volunteers from the audience who were having challenges in attracting and manifesting their desired outcome.

With each person that came up to the front of the room, I first checked the strength of their energy field and then checked to see what was undermining and blocking them from attracting their desired outcome. Although this process may seem complicated, it only took a few minutes to pinpoint the thoughts, attitudes, beliefs and unresolved traumas that were blocking each person. Explaining and releasing these took another few minutes.

During my talk and presentation, I was able to assist over a half dozen people to better understand and eliminate what was undermining their personal attraction and manifestation process. When they left the presentation, their energy was clear and aligned.

The Laws of Attraction and Manifestation always work perfectly — however to access and to gain the full benefit of these universal laws, we must be energetically clear and fully energetically aligned so that we allow these Laws to operate perfectly!

* * *

Back around 1995, I met a couple in London, England who owned the franchise for teaching the Bob Proctor Goal Setting Program. They were familiar with my work and wholeheartedly believed in my approach. To explore how my work would enhance their program, they invited me to attend one of their Goal Setting Programs. In this particular program all the attendees were very successful top corporate executives, entrepreneurs and business professionals.

As part of my agreement for attending, the franchise owners did not want me to tell anyone who I was or what I did until the final day of the program. On the last day of this program, when everyone was asked to stand in front of the room and to present their goals to the group, the owners asked me to "do my thing."

After each of these highly successful people read their goals to the room, I came up to the front of the room and, with their permission, checked their energy field to determine whether or not their written goals were actually what their heart and soul were counting on them to do. Said another way, I was checking whether their goals were in alignment with their soul purpose and soul essence.

After reading their energy field, I gave each person feedback as to what I was seeing, feeling and sensing about the congruity between what they had written as their goals, and what their soul was counting on them to do. To my amazement and to theirs — and to the entire group — not one person in the entire group really and truly wanted what they had written down as their goal. Based on what they had initially written as their goal, their soul, as well as the Laws of Attraction and Manifestation, would not wholeheartedly support them in achieving their goals.

After helping each of these very successful people identify their real heartfelt dreams, hopes, desires and goals, both the person I was assisting and everyone in the audience could sense, see and feel a marked change — there was a noticeable shift in the energy, appearance and attitude of the person I had just assisted. There was a tangible visible shift in each person's energy and physical appearance when his or her true SOUL GOALS were identified.

I specifically remember one extremely talented entrepreneur who had started five very successful high tech companies, only to sell them just before they became extremely profitable. The people who bought his companies made a fortune, however he was financially struggling. I was able to assist him in identifying and clearing the negative energy patterns and the reasons why he had sabotaged himself from reaping the financial benefits of his incredible talents.

It amazed me and everyone else in the program that although all of these people were highly educated and incredibly outwardly successful in their field of expertise, not one of them really wanted what they thought they wanted. As a result, their heart, body, mind and soul were not passionately excited about achieving their stated goals. You cannot easily reach your goals unless all aspects of you wholeheartedly support you in reaching your goals.

This experiment proved how important it is to have someone as part of your senior management team who can monitor the subtle energy patterns to make sure that entrepreneurs, business people and management stay totally focused and are on target — always hitting the bulls-eye — with their goals, business decisions, marketing plan, hiring, team building, pricing and all other aspects of their business. The small investment involved in hiring an experienced business coach who can intuitively read the energy patterns of the business could help eliminate many needless problems, while at the same time greatly improving the business's chances of success and higher profitability.

Chapter 9
Traumas, Wounds, Illness and Other Life Challenges

Illness and Disease

The primary reasons people get sick are: they are energetically blocked; they're not present in their physical body; they're out of balance or they're disconnected from their authentic selves. Most people who are ill are not being true to themselves. They are not paying attention to their thoughts, feelings and emotions, their body and spirit, or what their intuition and heart are telling them. The majority of health challenges (over 80%, according to my intuition) are simply energy blockages, where the deeper cause is an unresolved shock, trauma, loss, negative thought, attitude, belief, emotion, fear or hurt. The other 20% are caused or complicated by stress, dehydration, poor diet, nutritional challenges and other related issues. The body, like everything else, breaks down in the area of the greatest stress and pressure, and where the body's defenses are the weakest.

The specific illnesses we get are determined by our genetic weaknesses, which we inherit from our ancestors and the part of the physical body directly affected by those unresolved issues. In other words; the eyes are affected when we do not want to see or look at something; the ears are affected when we do not want to listen or hear something; the throat is affected when we do not speak our truth, or when we hold back communicating our knowing, and so on.

In my experience, almost all health issues people face, including learning disabilities, allergies, diabetes, hepatitis C and even cancer, are triggered by and are the result of mental, physical, emotional and spiritual energy blockages in the body.

Over the years, I have assisted clients suffering from lifelong, intense allergies (one totally healed in 45 seconds), hepatitis C (in one session), thyroid problems (one workshop), diabetes (in one session), and even the underlying mental, physical, emotional and spiritual cause of cancer (a few sessions).

Please note that I am not treating these people medically, nor do diagnose or prescribe. I am simply reading the person's energy field and assisting them to clear their energy blockages.

I have learned that it is not the illness or disease that is the real challenge; the only challenge lies in pinpointing the deepest root cause of what is throwing the body's energy field out of balance. Once the deepest root cause of the energy imbalance is identified and cleared, the body has the natural ability to come back into balance and heal itself. To accomplish this, I use my intuition to track the energy blockage back to the source — the deepest root cause of the health challenge.

Whether a person improves and totally heals — or not — is not up to me. Each person's soul is in charge, with some people's health greatly improving and even totally healing, while another person's health may not show any outward sign of improvement. It is important to remember that a person's mental, emotional, physical and even their spiritual well being may greatly transform, however there may be little or no apparent physical change in their health. In these cases, the person's karma and soul may be helped, healed and transformed, even though their physical health does not visibly show any signs of improvement. Remember that the soul always takes with it all that it has experienced, learned and achieved.

The Benefits of Illness and Disease

Illness and disease are warning signals and wake-up calls. Once the underlying cause has been addressed and healed, people often later call them great gifts! Illness and disease are strong indicators of what you have been avoiding and where your body has been compensating. Your body will keep adjusting and compensating until it finally reaches the breaking point where it cannot compensate any longer. When this happens, it will start giving you warning signs, demanding that you stop and pay attention. This often starts as whispers and then, over time, grows louder and louder. Normally, if we pay attention to the whispers, we can resolve most health issues fairly easily and quickly. However, if we do not listen and make the necessary changes, we will continue to get sicker and sicker until our physical body totally breaks down.

Unfortunately many people do not take holistic medicine, energy medicine, complementary therapies, healers or anything other than traditional Western medicine seriously. Most of us have been taught that Western medicine, pharmaceutical pills and surgeries are the only answer to solving all of our mental, emotional and physical health problems.

As a result, rather than taking an active role in their own healing process, most people have given their power and the responsibility for their health away to these mainstream methods. It's only when these interventions no longer have the answers and cannot help that people begin to take back their power, take personal responsibility for their own healing, and start to search for their own answers and solutions.

When traditional medical doctors admit that they cannot help any further and do not have answers, some people (at least, the wise ones!) start to take personal responsibility for themselves, searching, asking questions, and opening their minds to new ways of thinking and treating their health challenges. This search often opens people's minds to embracing a more holistic, metaphysical and spiritual perspective… and for many, this opens the doorway to their spiritual journey.

We need to keep ourselves both healthy and alive! Sometimes the medical profession has the answers and the spiritual healers do not, and vice versa. In recent history, the medical profession has not had the time, the training or the skills to determine the deepest root cause of a person's health challenges. Consequently, most present-day doctors deal with treating the patient's symptoms, rather than determining the deepest mental, physical, emotional and spiritual issues causing the energetic imbalance in the patient's body. Using my intuition, I can almost immediately pinpoint the deepest root cause of the energy imbalance causing a person's illness.

During my travels around the world, I was fortunate to spend many months in Greece, where I visited Delphi and a number of the ancient healing centers called Asclepions. I also spent time on the island of Cos, the location of the healing center of Hippocrates, a Greek physician often referred to as "The Father of Modern Medicine." In ancient times, these centers flourished.

As part of their treatment, healers used relaxation, diet, dream therapy, rest, good food, counseling and many other natural approaches still used by holistic healers and holistic medical practitioners today. The Eastern therapies (from China, India, etc.) have been using holistic methods for well over 6,000 years. Unfortunately, somewhere along the way, traditional Western medicine, with all of its specialization and testing, seems to have lost its awareness and sensitivity to the more expansive and all-inclusive holistic mind-body-spirit approach.

We have become trained to take a pill to deal with our feelings, emotions and issues rather than do deep emotional inner work to identify and release the deepest root cause of our unresolved hurt, pain, frustrations, fears and anxieties. Taking a pill, in most cases, simply numbs us, masks and suppresses our deeper challenges, deadens our aliveness and, because we have not dealt with the underlying issues, these unresolved issues fester and putrefy, poisoning our body. These unresolved emotions are the deepest root cause of almost all illnesses and diseases.

This difference in values, beliefs and approaches is one of the main reasons that a number of medical doctors and nurses split away from the more conservative and traditional American Medical Association and the American Nurses Association to form the more inclusive American Holistic Medical Association and the American Holistic Nurses Association.

* * *

A 63-year-old Australian woman named Karen came to see me for a private session. When I asked how I could serve her, she replied, "I have been treated for cancer and the medical doctors told me that they cannot do anything more for me. They sent me home to die, telling me that I have only 90 days to live. Can you help me?"

Immediately, I sensed that Karen really did not want to live. I sensed that about 15 years prior to our meeting, something had happened to break her spirit, and because of this, she had totally lost her will to live. I then asked her what significant traumatic event happened 15 years ago, to which she replied, "Nothing." Over and over I kept asking her what happened 15 years ago and she kept giving me the same answer.

I then asked her how long ago she had been diagnosed with cancer, to which she answered 12 years. Again, I repeatedly asked her what happened 15 years ago — and, finally, with a jolt, she remembered.

Fifteen years previously, she and her daughter had a huge fight, during which time her daughter told Karen that she never wanted to see her or talk to her ever again. After she shared this, I asked a key question: "Karen, when this happened, how did this make you FEEL?" Karen meekly answered: "I just wanted to die!"

Bingo! Within minutes of starting the session, we hit the nail on the head and discovered the deepest root cause of her cancer! The unresolved feeling of rejection, unworthiness, futility and anguish was the deepest root cause of her cancer.

I helped Karen to understand the link between her hurt, pain and feelings of loss on the one hand, and her unconscious manifestation of the cancer on the other. After one private session and one weekend workshop, she started glowing! During the workshop, Karen wrote her daughter a letter in which she forgave her and told her that she had a right to her own opinion — however that opinion really had nothing to do with Karen. When the workshop was over, Karen was radiant. When I intuitively checked out her energy, I could not see any signs of cancer anywhere in her body!

Karen's story demonstrates how important it is to discover and resolve the deepest root cause of your health or other life challenges. When working with a client, the first question I ask my intuition is, "What threw this client's energy field and their body out of balance, and allowed this health issue to manifest?" It is the answers I receive that help me to understand what I need to say, do or help clear in order to facilitate the necessary changes, breakthrough and healing.

* * *

Many years ago, a prestigious European cancer center contacted me, asking me to set up a new holistic residential retreat healing facility for them. They wanted me to bring in my own staff of healers and to supervise the entire medical staff. I happily agreed to work with them.

After I finished designing the entire program and they accepted it, I asked them a very profound question: "Rather than helping patients after they had surgery, chemotherapy and radiation, why not allow me to treat them with my techniques for a week or two before their surgery to see if we can get their tumors to shrink naturally? If the tumors shrank, we would continue to treat them using my methods. If the tumors grew, we would immediately refer them for surgery. And, if the tumors stayed the same size, we would consider each patient on a case-by-case basis.

This approach made total sense to me. "After all, why subject a patient to the trauma of surgery and then pump them full of highly toxic poisons (chemotherapy and radiation) if we can treat them naturally?" My concern was that we would have to work much harder to heal the patients after they were traumatized by the surgery and loaded with poisons.

The directors' response to what I knew was a brilliant and logical proposal was this: "There is not one doctor in this entire country who would believe that you can noticeably shrink a tumor in a week!" I was in shock because I knew from both my guidance and my experience that this was indeed possible! My answer was, "Well find me one!" As things turned out, because the economy slowed and financing dried up, I did not end up working for this organization.

In my heart and soul, I long for the day when I can assemble my own team of healers and medical professionals, so I can put all that I know into practice. I would also be honored to join an existing cutting-edge holistic medical practice or healing center.

People should not have to suffer. I know that when people face their issues and learn their lessons, the healings that result can be both profound and even instantaneous.

Traumas, Wounds and Soul Growth

It is said that our deepest, most painful wounds provide us with our greatest learnings and our most profound opportunities for soul growth. If we do not feel loved, safe or wanted as children, we might abandon and betray our true self, our authentic self. To survive, we might put on a mask, create a persona or even develop multiple personalities in order to survive and to fit in. All we want as children is to feel wanted, safe and accepted. At times, when we experience a shock, trauma or loss, we might shut down, or literally energetically leave our physical body to get away from and stop our pain.

When we shut down or leave our body, we abandon and betray our true self — our inner child — and move away from our authenticity. When we do this, we tend to become co-dependent and externally referenced, meaning we give away our power and knowing, and look to others for love, approval, answers and our identity, rather than to ourselves.

To be healthy, we have to reclaim our true self, our sacred personal power, our independence and our clarity. We have to learn to stay energetically present in our body, and to be independent, authentic and internally referenced.

***

In 1986, as I was driving from California to Alaska, I stayed in a small Canadian town for a few weeks while visiting friends. My friends introduced me to Kathy, a divorced woman, who was their close friend. One day I took Kathy and her two daughters, ages 5 and 7, to a park where we skipped stones across the lake and played on the swings.

Later that afternoon I took them into town for ice cream. The children excitedly ran back and forth in the store as they reviewed all the possibilities and constantly changed their minds about which flavor they wanted. Eventually each one made her choice.

When it came time for Kathy to choose a flavor, she went blank and could not tell me what flavor she wanted. I attempted to help her by asking her if she wanted a cup or a cone. Again she could not choose. Finally, I looked at her with deep compassion and asked what happened to her that she could not choose.

Eventually Kathy broke down in tears and told me her story. As a child, she would come home from school and witness her older brother and father fighting. Apparently, her older brother was rebellious and her father was a controlling alcoholic who would beat her brother until he was bloody. As a result, Kathy decided that the only way she could survive was to be invisible and to not have any thoughts, feelings or preferences of her own. By being invisible, she would not trigger her father's rage and she would, at least in her own mind, be safe.

Although this strategy kept her alive and safe, it broke her spirit and robbed her of her aliveness. Even though she was an adult when I met her and out of that toxic environment, she was still allowing herself to be dominated and controlled by her past history.

Karma

The word "karma" holds a lot of mystery and even triggers fear in some people. To me, karma is not a big deal. It's just like a set of balance scales. Some countries have the "Scales of Justice" as a symbol for their judicial system. Similarly, the concept of karma is all about balancing fairness, kindness, compassion, right action and learning our lessons.

Through our thoughts, actions and deeds, we either create positive, uplifting results by doing good deeds *(dharma)* or we create negative, ego self-serving results by doing selfish and bad deeds. It is very simple! My guides have often talked to me about my "cosmic bank account." Apparently, by having done a lot of good deeds in the past, I have accumulated a "positive cosmic bank balance" from which I can draw. If my actions had created a negative balance, a deficit, I would need to replenish my "account" with positive deeds and energies during this lifetime. We always have choice!

At a lower level of consciousness and spirituality, some see karma as being about duality: right/wrong, good/bad. However, at higher levels of consciousness and spirituality, it is only about learning — without any judgment at all.

The wheel of karma implies that if you do something wrong to someone or hurt them in any way, you have to come back and experience that person or another person, doing the same or similar type of wrong to you. The lesson is provided so you will know how it feels and you will choose to do things with more integrity next time. This awareness and learning balances the wheel of karma.

I have discovered and developed ways to greatly speed up the process of balancing karma by assisting clients to identify and fully learn their lessons. This allows clients to break free of their negative karmic patterns and transmute their karma in a matter of minutes, rather than lifetimes.

It is interesting to note that in Western cultures you are considered a hero when you save someone's life. Yet if you save a person's life in India, you would be thought to be interfering with that person's karma, and as a result you would be morally and financially responsible for that person's welfare for the rest of their life because you changed their fate — their karma.

We can also create karma when we betray ourselves, sacrifice ourselves inappropriately, or stay too long in an unhealthy or abusive relationship, job, marriage or country that does not honor our soul.

***

A long time ago, a very wise teacher of mine who was watching me as I was doing healings and assisting clients asked me, "Are you aware of what you are doing?" I replied that I only knew what I knew and asked what he was seeing. He said, "You are acting as a spiritual attorney, skillfully presenting your client's case to the Karmic Board. As you are presenting each case, you are negotiating, re-negotiating and clearing their karma: their karmic contracts."

Maybe this is why I and others, have sometimes seen sparks and flashes of light, as well as puffs of grey or black smoke coming off people while I assist them to clear and heal!

Karma is all about learning our lessons, changing and making positive changes in our life. Once we see things differently, change our ways and learn our lessons, there is no need for the karma (the imbalance) and it simply dissolves and melts away instantly.

Please note that I do not simply take away people's lessons. This would not help a person to learn, change or to grow. My gift is in my intuitive ability to clearly identify what the person's lessons are and then to explain these lessons to my client in such a way that he clearly understands them. Once the lessons are understood, my client then has the opportunity to make the required adjustments and changes in his thoughts, attitudes, beliefs and actions.

Clearing karma is really this easy!

Miscarriages, Abortions and Early Death

By communicating with the souls of deceased fetuses, children and young adults, I have learned many things. The following information is shared with sensitivity and deep compassion. Please keep an open mind and an open heart as you read this.

As a soul is infinitely wise, it already knows, even before it incarnates into a human body, whether the mother can and will carry the fetus full term or not. Please remember that prior to incarnating, each soul consciously chooses his major lessons and experiences, how long he will live and the type of life he will have. No one can ever kill a soul because every soul is eternal. From a soul perspective, the length of time a human lives is not important. What is important is for the person to gain the learning she desires or needs to progress on her current learning cycle.

Whenever I have intuitively communicated with the soul of a fetus that had died as a result of a miscarriage or a termination, I have never experienced the fetus being upset, angry, resentful or blaming the parents. In fact, the experience was just the opposite. The soul of the fetus was always grateful to her parents, especially her mother, for allowing her to connect to and experience the Earth's frequency and vibration — even if only for a little while.

Sometimes a soul just needs to come back for a short time, for a few days, weeks, months or years in order to learn, gain or complete something. The soul may also incarnate to provide an experience for their twin, siblings, parents or for the world. Some of these children choose to be role models, while others challenge the perceptions and reality of the world. Because of their bravery, these beings may touch the hearts and souls of thousands or even millions of people around the world due to their pain and suffering, or the way they face their challenges. Some children even challenge and transform the thinking of science, medical specialists and humanity.

Sticking Your Toe in the Water

Have you ever approached a lake or ocean to go swimming and started by sticking your big toe in the water to test how cold it was, only to then back away? Then you went back in up to your ankles and backed away again? Then you went in up to your legs, then up to your knees? Finally, you adjusted to the temperature of the water and went all the way in.

When a soul comes to the Earth plane, it does something similar. The dimensions where souls originate from vibrate at very high and pure energy frequencies. As the soul incarnates onto the Earth plane, the soul has to descend down into the heavy, dense, slow Earth frequency and vibration. This dramatic change in frequency, vibration and energy levels is like wading into cold water. This is very intense and requires a lot of adjustment on the part of a soul coming to Earth, especially during their first several Earth incarnations.

Many of the souls experiencing abortions and miscarriages are new to the Earth plane and are in the process of adjusting to the Earth's density. They purposely choose situations where they know they will only be alive for a few days, weeks, months or years. That is all they need as they are energetically adjusting to the Earth vibration. Eventually these souls adjust sufficiently where they can remain in a human body much longer.

You Might Have Been A Twin

In the mid 1990s, I learned that I had been a twin in the womb. Due to an accident my mother experienced, my twin sister's fetus had died when she was about 8-10 weeks old. My parents were never aware of my twin sister. When a psychic healer gave me this information, I grieved for months. The discovery explained certain feelings, emotions, sensitivities and fears I had felt for a long time. My unconscious guilt for not being able to protect and save my sister most likely triggered my burning desire to help, protect, guide, heal and educate people.

Since becoming aware of the existence of my twin sister, I have met a few other health professionals who have also discovered and studied this phenomenon. As I learned more about multiple embryos and fetuses, I started sensing and seeing this in people's energy fields. I learned that 20% or more of all single births have been twins or even triplets in the womb. Twins may have originally been triplets or more in the womb.

In almost all cases, the parents and the children are not consciously aware of the additional fetus. However, the emotional and energetic challenges that the surviving twin or triplet experiences are strong indicators that there was indeed another unborn child present.

As you read this section, if you had an emotional reaction, felt sadness or shed tears, your reaction could indicate that you were a twin in the womb.

* * *

The Story of Ben

Ben was a perfectly happy, healthy, vibrant and intelligent 8-year-old European boy who one day woke up and told his parents that he was going to die soon. He asked his parents to help him organize his funeral. They were shocked, of course, however Ben was so adamant about planning his funeral that they went along with it, not believing any of it. Ben joyfully proceeded to pick out his casket and the gravesite. He even gave his parents lists of the people he wanted them to invite to his funeral, the food he wanted to be served and the music he wanted played. Excited, Ben gave very specific details about everything, never showing any fear, sadness or regret.

A month later, the family left for a special overseas holiday trip. Near the end of the vacation, Ben got stung by a wasp, had an intense allergic reaction and quickly died. The family was in total shock. However Ben had already planned everything in minute detail and his funeral celebration went off exactly as he had asked.

This story shows how aware some people are of their destiny. Apparently, Ben did not need to live any longer in this incarnation. Although Ben's passing was a great blow to his parents, friends and loved ones, Ben's inner knowing and the plans he made for his own funeral prompted many people to question their perceptions about life, death, living, precognition and much more. Ben was definitely a catalyst for change.

I pray that this story brings peace, relief, understanding, self-forgiveness, self-compassion and healing to the parents and loved ones of children who have passed on.

Adjustments, Learning and Course Corrections

Almost all learning is a process that takes time, practice, patience and persistence. When children are born, they do not have the ability to walk, ride a bicycle, run a marathon or paint a picture perfectly. All talents and skills are learned and developed through incremental steps. A baby who is learning to walk first learns to crawl, then to stand with some assistance and then to stand without support. Eventually the baby begins to walk a few steps while holding onto someone. Then she takes a few wobbly steps and falls. Only after many tries does the toddler learn to stand and walk unassisted.

Did you know that airplanes, cruise ships, rocket ships and even guided missiles are off target 99.99% of the time? The only reason they land where they're supposed to land is because they continuously make course corrections. To course correct during your Earth journey, you have to pay attention, take total responsibility for yourself, be aware and take positive action.

Some people are perfectionists who refuse to start something new unless they can guarantee that they will do it perfectly the very first time they try. This is one of the main avoidance and procrastination excuses people use.

If you're one of those people who want to be perfect, be right and only do things flawlessly — good luck! Perfection is impossible to accomplish here on Earth. Just do the best you can in each and every moment, and keep making the course corrections that will keep you on target. The most important thing is to start, and then to continually polish, upgrade and fine-tune your creation or project. This is the absolute best you can do on Earth.

To speed your process and make things easier for yourself, seek out an intuitive healer, coach or mentor who can help you keep your energy field clear, stay focused, make better choices and keep you heading in the best direction.

Understanding Cycles

Almost everything in the universe operates in cycles of expansion and contraction — growth and decay. These cycles include the moon rotating around the Earth, the Earth circling the sun, the seasons, weather, tides, life and death, our biorhythms, life-force energy, the economy, love and much more. The phases of expansion and contraction exist in every cycle, however it's important to remember that no cycle or part of any cycle, is any better or worse than any other. They are all just elements of the bigger process.

Many women can tell you a lot about the changes in their body, emotions and moods as their menstrual cycle changes. What few people realize is that the cycles of the moon, along with other planetary movements, greatly affect everyone's energy and moods. The effects of these planetary influences are the basis of astrology. Add to this our individual biorhythms and you have a very interesting diverse mix of influences that affect each of us on a minute-to-minute basis, usually without our even realizing it.

The survival of early humans depended upon them being consciously attuned to the subtle changes in their surroundings, including the cycles of the seasons, the times of the year that plants, fruits and vegetables ripened, the mating habits and migration patterns of animals, and much more.

Even in our modern times, it is beneficial for us to be conscious of the cycles of life so we can be responsible on the one hand and flow with life's ups and downs, without being fearful or trying to control the process on the other hand. To expect to always feel good, and to be emotionally and financially on top of the world creates illusion, confusion, stress and depression. Cycles are natural occurrences.

We can create more suffering for ourselves when we take these cycles personally or go into fear, anger, hurt, regret, judgment, resentment or attempt to control a cycle. When we do, rather than staying centered and focused on adjusting to the changes and going with the flow, we can sabotage ourselves, as well as waste and deplete our energy.

Expansion and Contraction Cycles

We all experience cycles of expansion and contraction. In times of expansion, we are usually feeling good, making money, having opportunities, experiencing abundance, enjoying love in our lives and everything is going well for us. During these times, like when it's spring and summer, when the economy is expanding, when we are doing well and when the weather is bright and sunny, people feel better and are more positive. It feels like there's little to worry about and hardly anything to do except enjoy the abundance, relish the good times and maximize the opportunities.

On the other hand, during times of contraction, when we are not doing well, we may feel confused, angry, ill, sad, upset or depressed. These times are characterized by being unemployed or under employed. It may be a time when you've lost money or you don't have love in your life. No matter what the circumstances are, when you experience contraction in any area of life, you must stay positive, conscious and vigilant.

A contraction cycle, especially when it is a long-standing one, is a test of your patience and convictions, and of your ability to remain calm, focused and centered. Some people feel good as long as everything is going well. But the minute something happens that is not what they consider positive, they can mentally, emotionally and energetically crash. There is an expression I've heard people say about contraction times, and it is "hold on tightly and ride the tiger."

It's helpful to remember that cycles are absolutely normal. In fact, you can even benefit from them if you learn to be aware of them, accept them and learn how to adapt to them. For example, many people who live in Alaska during the summer avoid the long cold winters by moving to Hawaii, Florida or Palm Springs, California during the winter months. These people are affectionately referred to as snowbirds.

There are hidden benefits to the cycles. One overlooked benefit of the contraction cycle is in giving you time to rest, recharge, reflect, plan, organize and create projects that you can launch as the cycle shifts from contraction to expansion. If we use the time wisely — which can take a lot of trust, faith, discipline and commitment — we can prepare to take full advantage of the upcoming expansion. This is true regardless of whether a person is a farmer, a student, a businessperson or a real estate investor. We can also always grow in education, skills and knowledge.

Many cultures wisely stockpile food in the summer so they can have food in the winter, and many farmers repair their equipment in the winter so it will be ready for springtime. Similarly, when we understand, plan ahead, flow with the cycles, and use our time and resources shrewdly, we can greatly benefit from, and be equally comfortable with both the contraction and expansion cycles of life.

Resisting a cycle is insanity. We cannot expect every aspect of our life to be in a constant positive upswing of expansion. When we are in an expansion cycle, it is best to enjoy it and to flow with it. And when we are in a contraction cycle, we also have to learn to enjoy it and flow with it. Cycles are a natural and normal part of life.

It is extremely important to remember that the only constant in the entire universe is change!

Surviving The Bottom of a Contraction Cycle

As I've discussed, there are ways to survive and even to thrive during a time of contraction, a time when things are not going as well as we would like. The challenge is to stay conscious, remain open, positive, receptive, avoid blaming anyone and to never take things personally. It is also extremely important to keep focused on your goals, to continue to nurture and nourish yourself, and to keep moving forward in a positive direction, even if you can only take baby steps. When in a down cycle, this can take immense courage.

Keeping a strong positive mental attitude will help you to adapt and survive during cycles of contraction. No matter how bad things may seem, choose to take positive actions to keep your mental, physical, emotional and spiritual energies as clear and positive as possible. This is especially true when you feel down, stuck, confused, disoriented, depressed and when you feel like things just don't seem to make any sense.

When slight negative mood changes occur, it is fairly easy to shake them off. However, when deeper mood changes and depression affect us, it is very helpful to have a support system in place to help. Unfortunately, many people turn to prescription drugs, alcohol and recreational drugs to numb their feelings and emotions. It is important to remember that there are other, more helpful ways to shift your energy into a positive direction.

If you find that your energy is weak and you cannot understand why you feel the way you do, you might have picked up some negative energies in your energy field that are scrambling and depleting your energy. Whenever you are feeling down or depressed, do your best to resolve the issues on your own. If you cannot clear your energy or snap out of feeling negative within a few days, then it may be a good time to contact a good intuitive healer, coach or mentor who can read your energy, give you insights into what is really going on in your life and energetically clear your energy field. Providing guidance and clearing out these discordant energies are two of my specialties. Once your energy field is cleared, you will have more positive energy and greater clarity.

The Dark Night of the Soul

The Dark Night of the Soul is the phrase used to describe what we experience when we find ourselves at the absolute bottom of an extreme downward cycle. It's when a person is lost in the depths of despair and feels abandoned, betrayed, isolated, alone, hopeless, helpless, confused, frustrated and lost. It's when someone feels overwhelmed, depressed, out of control and cannot find any path forward. It is a time of being intensely tested since, by definition, the person has lost all faith, trust, courage, confidence and direction. They may have also lost all of their self-worth, self-esteem and they may feel like they are unworthy. They may also feel like they have nothing to live for. Eventually, most of us will face this challenge. Some of us have faced this depth of despair a number of times. I know I have. During such an extreme low point, the person must choose between giving up or entering into a time of deep personal introspection and change. This shedding of the old ways of existing and embracing new positive strategies leads to renewed expansion and soul growth.

Even with all of my education, experience and abilities, I look back on the dozen or more times in my life when I felt so exhausted, battered and frustrated that I barely had the strength to take even one more breath. I remember times in my life when I just wanted to give up and end it all. I felt useless and worthless, and believed I was a total failure. I have cried out in sheer frustration, "God, why have you opened my eyes and given me these precious gifts? Please open the doorways so that I can do my work!"

There were also times when I felt so alone, lonely, isolated and misunderstood that everything seemed utterly hopeless. Looking back, I can now see that although these times were excruciatingly painful, each low point held the hidden seeds for my next level of learning, expansion and soul growth. These were times when my rough edges were being polished and my skills were being honed.

In many ways we all start out like rough uncut diamonds that are then cut, polished and placed in settings, to best show our magnificence.

Unfortunately, many people mistakenly and naively believe that the spiritual path is a bed of roses, and expect everything to be blessed and easy. This is the furthest thing from the truth. Every spiritual person I know has gone through gut-wrenching tests, trials and losses that have shaken them to the very core of their being. Some have faced financial challenges; others have had relationship challenges, suffered the loss of loved ones or dealt with life threatening illness. Few, if any, have had an easy life. Facing these challenges gifts us with greater knowledge and a deeper understanding of ourselves, of life and of the challenges that we humans face. It also provides the life experiences and knowledge we need so we can gain compassion, understanding and help others.

As I am frequently assisting, people, companies and organizations in crisis, I am well aware of the amount of positive energy and support that people in crisis require. We are living in a time of great change and uncertainty, when all of us are being severely challenged by the massive social, political, economic, financial and planetary energy shifts now occurring. And this is only the beginning of what is to come in the near future. We must prepare ourselves now, so we will be internally strong enough to cope with the many changes and challenges that are ahead of us.

Someone I know once said, "The greatest sin is the failure to risk, stretch, learn, change and grow." We face many tests and challenges in life. How we deal with these adversities — by either gracefully embracing them or by shutting down and running away from them — will determine our rate of soul growth. If you surrender into and learn your lessons, you will grow. And if not, you become ensnared and crippled by your own fear, denial and resistance. Remember, if you fail to learn your lessons now, you will have to return and face them again either later in this lifetime or in your next incarnation! Isn't it better to face your issues now, to deal with them and to pass your tests now?

Most of the world's greatest masters, prophets, leaders, teachers and healers have spent time wandering alone in either an inner or outer wilderness. They were severely tested. They struggled with their ego/personality, faced their innermost fears and insecurities, and finally they learned to listen to their inner voice, their intuition, the voice of Spirit.

Once they returned from their inner battles in the wilderness, many of these great enlightened beings offered their wisdom, insights, gifts and services to their communities and to the world. Just like them, the rest of us who wander in our own wilderness are also being tested. We are being challenged to continue stretching, learning, changing and evolving.

Terminating one's own life is never a good solution. Even if a person does end his own life, he will just have to come back again and face the same challenges he was avoiding in this lifetime. Some teachings even say that a person who takes their own life will have to face their original challenges, plus will have a few more challenges added on when he reincarnates again.

The truth is, ***we are never allowed to choose — and are never given — more or bigger challenges than we can handle. That is the Universal Law.***

Should you be open, receptive, desire and be willing to accept help and support, there are many highly qualified people who specialize in assisting those who are going through a challenging process and are in crisis.

Please know that you are important and that your life matters! I highly encourage you to make sure you get the help and support you need, even before your life gets to the crisis stage. Many world-class healers have been through this too, sometimes more than once, so we know what you are going through.

In light of the many new energies coming into Earth and the many people who are in crisis seeking assistance, you might also consider getting together with other like-minded lightworkers to learn, teach, support and heal each other. You can do healing sessions in teams. Many very spiritual groups, such as the Essenes in the Middle East (around 100 BC) and the Cathars in southern France (12th to 14th century), were spiritual communities whose members studied, travelled, taught and supported each other.

* * *

The Benefits of Forest Fires

The United States Forestry Service used to put out forest fires as fast as possible. More recently, they have learned that they have been unwittingly creating a problem by doing so. When a forest fire breaks out, it burns away the accumulated dead undergrowth and ground debris that prevents the new growth and the healthy development of the forest from happening.

This is a lot like what happens when we go through the dark night of the soul. The burning off, clearing out and letting go process can be very scary and painful, however, after we go through it and come out the other side, we are revitalized, and are on new higher ground. Note: some people go through the dark night of the soul more than once. The key to surviving it is to be kind, gentle and compassionate with yourself, to stay present, stay focused, keep doing what needs to get done, love yourself, and seek help and support.

* * *

The Suicide of a British Healer

A number of years ago, without warning, a well-known British healer took his own life. When the news came out, many people asked, "How could this have happened to an experienced healer? What went so wrong that someone who helped so many people would take his own life? Why didn't he reach out for help? Aren't healers above this? How could this have been prevented? Why? Why? Why?"

His passing left many unanswered questions, and left people in a state of shock and confusion.

The morning after hearing the news, I woke up knowing that I needed to write an article about the important lessons this tragic event had to teach us: we need to make sure that people receive help well before they fall victim to life's challenges. I knew that his cry for help was either not clearly communicated, not properly received or both.

The lessons the healer who took his life gifted to us are profound — If only we are willing to learn from them. His message is that everyone, especially those of us who are healers, therapists, counselors and psychics, who are constantly giving, helping and taking care of other people, must learn to love, honor, respect and support ourselves. We must also learn to reach out to each other, to clearly communicate, ask for help, ask for support and to give support to each other, especially in times of need. It is much better than just a good idea; it is rewarding for both the person asking for help and the person giving the support.

One of my greatest joys in life is helping, supporting and teaching others through my private sessions, coaching, trainings and apprenticeship programs. When I reach out to others for support, it also gives them an opportunity to feel wanted, needed and important. This mutual support and sharing of skills allows us to bond with and learn from each other.

* * *

Choosing to End One's Life Early

John was a European man in his late 60s who had lost his beloved sister and was deeply saddened by her passing. They had enjoyed a special bond between them. After his sister passed, John's health took an unexpected turn for the worst and deteriorated rapidly. Although prior to his sister's death he had been in good health and he seemed to have many good years ahead of him, I could sense that once his sister died, he had made a decision to end this lifetime early so he could join his sister in spirit.

Whether or not he will actually meet his sister in spirit is not up to me. Beings on the other side determine that kind of thing. Once John made his decision to go, he was no longer open, receptive or responsive to the healing energy that I sent to him. It was obvious that he had made a choice to end his life early, and his health deteriorated rapidly.

One of the hardest lessons for me this lifetime was to learn to allow people to choose what was right for them, without my attempting to influence their decisions and choices — unless they specifically asked for my opinion, help and support.

* * *

Choosing To Change, Heal and Continue Living

An Asian couple in their early 50s came to see me for a joint session. As we talked about their life and children, I suddenly stopped them and asked for more information about their 16 year-old daughter. Although they kept telling me that she was fine, I intuitively sensed that she needed to see me immediately. Seldom had I ever experienced such a strong sense of urgency. When I shared this with her parents, they laughed and said that their daughter was not open or receptive to the kind of healing work that I did. Upon my insistence, they agreed to talk with her when they got home.

The next day she arrived with her father. After a short conversation to make sure she was comfortable doing a session with me, we started. Usually I do not see a minor without a parent present, however in this case the father agreed to wait outside.

Shortly after the session began, I asked her if she was planning to kill herself. She burst into tears and admitted that she had already written her suicide note and had been planning on taking her life that same week. We spent the rest of the session discussing the specific changes she needed to make in her life in order for her to commit to staying alive. I also asked her what support she needed from her parents?

Towards the end of the session, I asked if she felt safe enough and comfortable enough for her father to join us in the session. With my support, she did. When she spoke to her father, he had no idea of how distraught his daughter had been or that she had planned on taking her life that same week. They agreed to talk more openly and honestly, and to make sure she had all the support she needed.

Over the decades, I have been privileged to assist many teenagers, young adults and adults who felt like they were alone, had no one to talk to, no place to turn to, did not feel loved or understood, were depressed, and were ready to give up and end their lives. Fortunately, I am frequently able to intuitively pick up this information, tune into their feelings and emotions, and assist people through their challenges. Please know that you are never alone. There are many people who care deeply about you and who have the skills to help you, and your loved ones, through the dark, challenging periods of your life!

* * *

The Burning Ember

Many years ago, I heard a story that touched me deeply. It was about a very religious Jewish man named Avraham, who stopped attending synagogue. When the Rabbi went to visit Avraham at his home, Avraham argued that he could study and pray alone, and did not need to go to the Temple. After much passionate discussion, they both became very quiet. After sitting in silence for a long time, both staring at the glowing, crackling fire in the fireplace, the Rabbi quietly got up and went over to the fire.

Using the small shovel beside the fireplace, he took the biggest and brightest glowing ember out of the fire and placed it on the bricks, slightly away from the main fire. Then he sat back down. A few minutes later, this bright glowing ember dimmed and went out. Nothing further was said that evening. The next week, Avraham returned to the synagogue.

The moral of the story is that even the brightest ember will go out without the support of the other hot embers. We all need each other for help, support, friendship, sharing, learning, changing and growing. We all need friends, support and community, especially as we get older!

Please have the courage to reach out for help and support whenever you feel the need, and especially before things get bad. An ounce of prevention is a good thing! If you feel you need help, assistance, guidance or just someone to talk to, please reach out immediately. You are worth it and you deserve to be supported!

Extremely Challenging Lifetimes

We all know people who have or are experiencing tremendous challenges in their lives, like dealing with physical abuse, sexual abuse, addictions, living in a war zone, being born into an abusive household, being in an abusive relationship, or other difficult and violent situations.

From a soul perspective, these people are advanced souls who, before coming to Earth, have consciously chosen to take on extremely challenging situations. I know of women who were born into a family where, had they not attracted their father's attention and sexual abuse, all of the other daughters in the family would have been badly sexually abused. These brave women made the soul choice to purposely attract all their father's attention and abuse so their sisters would be safe.

I know other people who were born into families where abuse was passed down from one generation to the next for many generations. In a lot of these families, the abuse was accepted and considered both natural and normal. Using their strength and courage, these advanced souls stepped in and stopped the abuse from happening in this lifetime, and from being passed down to future generations.

Taking on these challenges is not for the fainthearted. It requires tremendous courage. It is only taken on by advanced souls who are committed to stopping abuse, and to bringing more light and love into their family system, and onto the planet.

Energy Blockages

An energy blockage occurs whenever the body's natural energy flow is scrambled, restricted, partially blocked or completely shut down. A good example of this is when you get scared and hold your breath. If you hold your breath too long, you pass out. However, even when you pass out, your body is still designed to automatically start breathing again. Humans are perfectly programmed to survive and prosper.

Unfortunately, when you shut down energetically, there is no one and nothing to remind you that after the danger has passed, it is safe and okay to open back up again. Our mind and body have no automatic instantaneous way of releasing trauma. So trauma can become trapped and stored in the mental, physical, emotional and spiritual body, as well as in the conscious and subconscious mind. It is important to be aware that, depending upon the nature of the trauma and the sensitivity of the person, even one experience can cause long-term debilitating effects. This is what Post Traumatic Stress Syndrome (PTSD) is.

PTSD is widely recognized as being associated with the unresolved trauma experienced by military combat personnel. What is not as well known is that men, women and even children who have been raised in abusive or dysfunctional families, or who live in those types of environments, also usually exhibit the exact same traits.

The shutting-down reflex is compounded, reinforced and complicated when multiple traumatic events occur. Even though people shut down in an attempt to protect themselves and to remain safe, shutting down emotionally and energetically can build energy blockages in the body, which can in turn cause many further life challenges.

There are an infinite number of and countless types of energy blockages we may experience. They can undermine your ability to relax, be happy, enjoy life, stay focused, trust people, create prosperity, develop healthy relationships and be intimate. On the mental level, energy blockages can distort the thinking process and the way the mind works. They can include negative thoughts, attitudes, beliefs, fears, insecurities and conscious or unconscious memories. They can occur on the emotional level too, showing up as inabilities to connect to our authentic feelings and emotions, create healthy relationships, set appropriate boundaries, stay grounded and centered, feel safe and secure, or to trust the process of life and living. Physical blockages might include a health issue or skeletal structure challenge, the inability to digest food, maintain organ functioning, walk properly, be coordinated or play sports well.

Spiritual blockages might include the inability to connect with one's intuition, inner guidance, or guides and teachers.

Blockages can also take the form of inappropriate or outdated psychic cords (energy connections) and energetic attachments to people, places or things. Energy blockages can also come in the form of health challenges or in one's inability to manifest and create your desired results. Blockages can create irrational fears of water, people, closed places, spiders, snakes, flying and more.

All of these blockages can be the result of a real or imagined threat or trauma. I have found that the trauma you are experiencing might not even have been your trauma. It could have been your mother's, father's or someone else's. To the person experiencing an unresolved trauma or blockage, regardless of the source, it all seems very real and sabotages their quality of life.

When a client is ready, open, willing, receptive and committed, the energetic cause of the blockages and challenges can be intuitively identified and released, usually within one session.

Chapter 10
The Bigger Picture

Creative Visualization, The Law of Attraction and Manifestation

The greatest roadblock to manifesting our desires in life is the lack of clarity and alignment of our conscious and unconscious thoughts, feelings, attitudes, beliefs and emotions. Just as it is much easier to create a pinpoint of light using a laser beam than it is with a floodlight or a searchlight, it is also much easier to manifest our desires when all of our conscious and unconscious thoughts, feelings and emotions are crystal clear, fully aligned and totally focused. The clearer, more aligned and focused they are on a mental, physical, emotional and spiritual level, the faster and more complete our manifestation will be.

It is no wonder that instant manifestation is so difficult to achieve when you consider the many factors involved. The dense and scrambled energy of the Earth plane, each individual's conscious and unconscious fears, negative thoughts, any low self-image and self-esteem that people carry, and their limiting beliefs — all of these get in the way of creating easy manifestation here on Earth.

Manifesting occurs more easily when we focus solely on the end result we desire, seeing, feeling and experiencing it as if it has already happened. It is important for us to relax, trust the process, and not be worried or concerned about the details or the process. Our job in the manifestation process is to figure out exactly what we desire and to imagine ourselves as already having received it. It is the universe's job to handle all the details required to fulfill our desires, and to deliver exactly what we requested.

It is interesting to note that when intuitive and psychic people observe the energetic holographic image of any plant or tree seed, all they see is the energetic blueprint of the full-grown mature plant or tree. They never see the blueprint of the tiny seed or of any of the stages the seed will go through as it grows into its final fully developed form. Understanding this is one of the keys to manifestation. Focus only on seeing the perfectly delivered end result.

Likewise, within each of us and within everything we wish to manifest, the blueprint of our final fully matured expression already exists. This is where we need to focus all of our thought energy. Understanding this is one of the key secrets to activating The Law of Attraction, manifestation and healing.

The secret is to clearly identify what is truly desired and then to eliminate all mental, emotional, physical and spiritual, conscious and unconscious sabotage patterns that are undermining this process. Should you experience challenges in manifesting your desires, clearing and aligning the energy can usually be accomplished in a single session.

Note: There is a free download on my website, that describes this process more fully.

Appearances and Illusions

When people who are struggling financially see very wealthy people, they tend to feel envious. And when they see a person living in the streets, such as an alcoholic, drug addict or prostitute, they tend to look down upon them. Yet, over the years, I have learned that those who take on the hardest and most difficult challenges in life are often the most advanced spiritual souls, and are frequently true masters. On the other hand, many of the people caught up in the game of money, power, sex and religion are actually less advanced souls, are not balanced, and are still learning about the right use of will and power.

Regardless of outward appearance, status or financial wealth, each one of us is exactly where we are supposed to be, learning the perfect lessons we need to learn in order for us to evolve. Everything that we attract and experience is dependent upon what our specific soul lessons are.

Many years ago, I led a workshop in a major European city where three of the 22 attendees were multi-millionaires. During the two days of the workshop, these three people cried many more times than any of the other workshop participants. Just because they had material wealth did not mean their lives were easy, pain free or that they were happy. As they cried, they were releasing and healing the tremendous deep-seated hurt, pain and trauma they had been carrying.

A large percentage of the world population has learned to suppress their true feelings, emotions, hurt, anger, pain and tears. Blocking authentic feelings and emotions takes a lot of energy. Trapped energy robs people of their health, wellbeing, spontaneity, aliveness, joy, happiness, intuition, creativity and life force. Trapped and blocked energy is the main cause of low energy, depression, illness and disease.

* * *

Before leaving for my first trip to Asia, one of my wise women colleagues gave me a very stern warning. She said, "Michael, stay very conscious. And remember, regardless of what you are seeing, you are always looking at God, at Spirit expressing!" This strong warning helped me to stay centered when I experienced the poverty, pain and suffering I saw on that trip. It allowed me to see the people and the world in an entirely different light. My wise and respected friend warned me because she knew I was very sensitive and empathic. She was protecting my heart.

One day, as I walked alone in the large Bangkok, Thailand open market, I noticed a young man on a skateboard heading in my direction. He had no legs and was sitting on his skateboard. With gloved hands he skillfully propelled himself, winding in and around the numerous stalls. All of a sudden our eyes met. In that instant, he gave me a huge smile and the thumbs up sign. It was as if we had known each other forever and were best friends meeting once again.

My heart opened as I smiled back, nodded my head in recognition of his perfect soul and returned his thumbs up. Seconds later, he whizzed past me, never stopping to ask for money. I will always remember this "meeting and respecting of two souls." Even now as I write, this beautiful memory brings tears to my eyes. And it also triggered major goose bumps in my book editor!

The Mirror Effect

When you get up in the morning, do you brush the mirror or do you brush your hair? If you are a woman, do you put make-up on the mirror or on your face? If you are a man, do you shave the reflection of your whiskers in the mirror or do you shave your face? Of course not. But many people live their entire lives attempting to control and change the outside world rather than deeply connecting with and changing themselves. Attempting to control or change the outside world is about as effective, and makes as much sense as shaving the mirror. Doing the deep inner healing work is the real key to learning, changing and growing, so you can truly experience joy, happiness, ease and grace.

The external world you see and everything you attract are mirror reflections of your conscious and unconscious internal thoughts, feelings, attitudes, beliefs and values. If you really and truly wish to know where you are in life, just watch what you are attracting and how you are feeling about yourself. Or — even better, enter into a romantic relationship and you will get to see exactly how open, receptive, kind, caring, generous, flexible and loving you are!

Each of us is like a radio tower with multiple broadcasting satellite dishes. From the first dish (the conscious mind) we send out a strong, clear signal that we want to be loved, happy, successful and prosperous. From an external perspective, it appears that our thoughts and desires are very pure, clear and aligned. However, unknown to us, we also have a number of subconscious (or "unconscious") broadcasting dishes that are less obvious than the first. These messages are being sent by our subconscious mind.

Without your knowing it, your subconscious mind may be broadcasting self-limiting messages that greatly contradict — and can even completely negate — the positive desires and message of your conscious mind. It might be: "I really honor my father, who is less successful than I am and I really do not want to outshine him. So I will stay small." Or: "I am not perfect and if I become really successful, my imperfection will be found out. So I will try and try and try very hard, however I will only play small and I won't allow myself to be placed in a situation where I can fail." Or: "In a past life, I was in strict religious orders that did not condone my being happy, successful or in a loving relationship. If I allow myself to be happy, successful and loved, I will be betraying the vows I took back then." These are just a few of the many possible unconscious thoughts that can sabotage our attracting joy, happiness, love, abundance, success and much more.

The subconscious mind may hold other limiting beliefs, too, such as: "I cannot be both successful and spiritual. So, allowing myself to be happy, to be successful and to be in a fantastic relationship will mean giving up my spiritual path. Life is about either/or and not having both. So I have to choose one over the other in this lifetime." Or: "If I allow myself to enjoy the Earth experience too much, I might get trapped here! I must not be too happy or successful here." Or we may be limited by past life religious vows: "My job is to sacrifice myself, to serve and take care of others, so my having love, happiness, abundance and enjoying what I am doing is not possible."

These are only a few examples of the many self-sabotaging messages that exist in our subconscious mind, well below the level of our conscious awareness. Healing and transforming these are an important, if not critical, part of our Earth journey. Using my intuition, I can easily track, identify and assist my clients to eliminate these deep-seated unconscious, self-sabotaging, negative thoughts, attitudes, beliefs, fears, memories and patterns. Healing and transforming these automatically greatly improves a person's relationships, financial success and frees them to be happier, more fulfilled and more aligned with their soul purpose. Once cleared, people are in a much better position to be open to being more successful, to creating greater abundance, and to authentically expressing who they truly are.

Resistance

Resistance and hesitancy are not bad things. When you experience resistance, it is a signal that some part of you is feeling uncomfortable, unsure or unsafe. Whenever you feel resistance, it is important for you to pay attention. Resistance can range from mild reluctance — a hesitancy or unwillingness to do something — to an extremely overwhelming, life-threatening, paralyzing fear. Resistance may mean a variety of things. When you accurately interpret and understand your feelings, emotions and reactions, they can guide you in the best direction, as well as accelerate and enhance your soul growth. However, if you don't interpret them correctly, they can become overwhelming, confusing, limiting, destructive and even debilitating.

Imagine going on your first date, taking your first job, going away to college, going on your first road trip alone, buying your first car, getting married or buying your first house. All of these can be very positive life-affirming activities, however, they often still bring up loads of doubts, fears, insecurities and hesitation. Whenever we stretch beyond our current comfort zone, it is both natural and normal for us to experience some butterflies and anxieties. The best way to approach these situations is to be open, receptive, curious and willing to embrace new experiences. It is also important to make sure that you take full responsibility for making sure that you feel safe and supported. Before making any major decision, it is important to do your research and to make sure that you feel comfortable with the choices you are making.

In order to experience life fully, you must stay energetically present and take the positive opportunities presented to you for learning, changing and growing. Avoiding positive growth opportunities will only undermine your soul growth — which will take you on another, less desirable, path of learning.

There are two types of resistance. The first occurs when your intuition, soul and your spirit, are accurately warning you of a real danger or that something is not right for you. The second comes from your limited human ego and personality as it fights for survival and control, only wanting things to stay the same. This type of resistance can be triggered whenever you challenge an old limiting belief system, attempt to break free of an old habit pattern or step onto new ground. If it's your first time doing anything, it is perfectly natural and normal for you to feel unsure of yourself. Insecurity, uncertainty, shyness, lack of experience and perfectionism can easily bring up hesitation and resistance. There are often times when resistance occurs even though you really want to move forward and stretch, learn, change, grow and break free.

The first type of resistance happens when your soul and spirit warn you of danger, or tries to signal you that you are heading in the wrong direction. It wants to protect you from harm and keep you alive. In these situations, fear and resistance can be strong positive warning signs that something is not right and that you should consider your options carefully.

Warning signs like these can show up when you are looking to buy a car, rent an apartment, go out on a date or take a vacation. With practice, you will learn to sense the difference between a true warning signal, which is usually pretty strong and the feeling that comes when you are just stretching beyond your existing comfort zone.

Our minds and bodies are neurologically programmed to keep us safe and out of harms way. So when it seems like we might do something that is new for us, or if we are doing something that may cause us harm, our mind/body system might go into resistance. It is normal and natural for the ego and personality to want to maintain control and to stay with what they know, what is comfortable and what they have been programmed to do. At the same time, our soul, spirit, intuition and heart keep encouraging us to stretch, expand, learn, change, grow, risk and evolve. When this happens, an internal battle between our ego and personality on the one hand, and our soul on the other, occurs.

The challenge with dealing with resistance is to accurately interpret and respond to the feelings, emotions and warning signals you get. It is extremely important to know what the trigger is and why you are feeling resistant. It is also important to understand whether the resistance represents a warning message from your soul to back off and protect yourself, or whether it represents your soul calling on you — counting on you — to push through the resistance so you can get to the positive expansion on the other side of it.

Is it your ego and personality talking to you, wanting to limit you and keep you small? Or is it your soul trying to get your attention? Knowing the source and the energetic difference between these two signals is crucial to your soul growth.

In order to differentiate between the two, it is helpful to ask yourself a few questions:

1) What event, action, thought or emotion triggered the feeling of resistance?

Usually, the trigger is a change in your normal interactions that takes you out of your comfort zone, and is significant enough to wake up and trigger your internal alarm bells. If the change was small or meaningless, the alarm bells would not have been set off. For you to be triggered, something had to activate your neurological defense system. There is no need for judgment when this happens; only the awareness that something has shifted or is in the process of shifting.

2) What part of you is sending out the warning message?

If the warning message is coming from your survival instincts, such as fear, your mind, ego, personality, history or programming and you surrender to the resistance, you will most likely be sabotaging yourself and holding yourself back. If you continue to back off, limit yourself and allow your ego and personality to dominate and control you, you may be setting yourself up for a lifelong pattern of playing small, being invisible and settling in life, without ever really living up to your full potential. However, if the warning message is coming from your soul, your guides, teachers, higher levels of consciousness or your intuition, then it is important to listen and pay attention. Discerning the difference between these is the key.

3) What is the true purpose of the warning message?

The true purpose of any warning message is to let you know that you are experiencing change and that some part of you is concerned that the change might not be good for you. Whenever your perception of reality changes, you might feel discomfort, uncertainty or even fear. Or, you might feel excitement and a sense of aliveness.

I am amazed at how many people on vacation are open, receptive, curious and adventuresome. Yet when these same people return home, they once again become inactive, unwilling to take risks and are closed to living life fully!

4) What is the best response to a warning message of resistance?

Since both types of resistance energetically feel very similar, it's not always easy to accurately discern which one is coming up. Unfortunately, simply feeling the feeling won't likely give you the information you need. Discerning the true source of the resistance requires tremendous self-awareness and self-honesty. If you can't determine the true source of your resistance on your own, it is advisable to find an experienced intuitive healer who can track your energy, determine the source of the resistance, help you to resolve your uneasiness and get you back on track.

No matter where the resistance is coming from, you can always make a conscious choice to relax, breathe, bless and release your old limiting programming.

* * *

Resistance When Making Quantum Leaps of Faith

There have been times in my life when tremendous fears and insecurities have challenged me and come up for me to face. One of those times was in 1986, when I was about to leave on a summer-long camping trip and drive from Palm Springs, California to Fairbanks, Alaska. The fear was so strong that it was debilitating, that is until I finally knew I had to make a decision. At that point, I took a deep breath, got in my car and started driving. After driving only about 15 miles, the energy totally shifted, everything lightened up and I started laughing and singing, "I am off to see the wizard." The trip lasted six months.

* * *

In 2005, I was about to take a trip from England to several countries, including Nepal, Thailand, Hong Kong, Malaysia, Singapore, Australia and New Zealand. I did not know many people, was short on money and knew that I would have to rely on my credit cards to sustain me. My fears and insecurities were immense until a stranger from Australia emailed me, and said that she had heard that I was coming in that direction and offered assistance. As she used to be a travel agent, she was able to give me suggestions, which gave me the courage and confidence to take the leap of faith I needed. The trip, which I extended to nine months, was an incredible success. It also opened up many new spiritual connections, business opportunities and lifelong friendships for me.

* * *

Resistance When Running Cross-Country

I experienced a lot of intense feelings of resistance when I was in high school, training for and running the 2 1/2 mile cross-country events. At times, the pain became so great that every muscle in my body ached severely and I felt like my lungs would burst. However, I soon learned that if I ran just a little further, all of the pain and resistance would vanish. This breakthrough is often referred to as getting your "second wind" — and once that barrier is broken, all the pain and resistance quickly melt away. This experience taught me that the human body gives many intense signals for runners to stop and give up. However by pushing through those signals, runners can go far beyond their previous resistance limits. This is true in life, too.

* * *

Energy Shifts

On November 11, 2011, I was at my cousin's house in Southern California, talking on the phone, when all of a sudden I felt an energy shift that left me so weak, empty and completely exhausted that I did not care if I lived or died. It felt as if someone had pulled a plug, like the drain in a bathtub and all of my energy had drained out of me. I immediately called several of my most trusted friends and asked for their assistance to stabilize my energy.

Shortly thereafter, I flew to New Zealand where a beloved and trusted friend, Jasmail, a Sikh, took one look at me and had me lay down on his living room couch. For the next two months he slowly nursed me back to health. This energy shift literally knocked me off my feet; I barely had the energy to walk to the bathroom and make it back to the couch where I slept. Jasmail fed me, rubbed my feet, prayed over me, and taught me what true service and unconditional love are.

When I was finally able to go outside for a very slow short walk, I was so oversensitive and so scared that I needed him to stay right by my side, or else I would go into a panic. I didn't realize it at the time, however I later learned that

I was going through a very positive shift, and was experiencing an upgrade in my energy and consciousness!

When I told Jasmail how scared I was about everything, he laughed at me, knowing that what I was going through was just a cleansing, a clearing out process, a spiritual initiation and that once I came out the other side, it would provide me with greater clarity and additional spiritual gifts so that I could help others in need. He was absolutely certain of this; yet I was so overwhelmed and lost in the fog of the process I was going through that I could not see or even imagine any of this.

A few months later, my energy returned and I was able to start teaching again, which I did from a higher plane of consciousness. This cleansing and rebirthing process has happened to me a number of times in this lifetime.

Going through this process of stripping away the old and building the new is extremely challenging, especially for someone who is used to being independent, in control, giving, taking care of and doing for others.

Without Jasmail's help, love, support and wisdom, I have no idea what would have happened to me. There are many Beings of Light assisting us on this planet — some in human form. I cannot thank or honor Jasmail enough. I have no idea what would have happened to me had he not been there at the precise time I needed support.

* * *

Very few people — not even highly skilled doctors or medical professionals — understand a spiritual breakthrough and the integration process that goes with it. Even fewer people have the first hand experience and know how to help people going through this spiritual birthing process, and the dimensional doorways that open during such experiences. Without significant experience, knowledge and spiritual assistance to guide you through such occurrences, you could end up being considered mentally, physically or emotionally unstable by the medical and psychiatric community.

Confusion

There are two types of confusion. The first kind of confusion is the healthy, normal, natural confusion of being in a new place, on new ground, with new sets of rules. Confusion naturally happens when a person has to adjust to new circumstances, rules, surroundings, interaction patterns and/or new ways of being.

The second type of confusion happens when someone consciously or unconsciously uses confusion and fear as a form of avoidance and protection. Here a person uses confusion to limit and to hold himself back. Fear of making a decision, fear of moving forward, resistance and perfectionism are a few causes of this type of confusion.

Healing

My definition of healing is very broad and all-inclusive. For me, healing is simply the act of improving either one's own or another person's mental, physical, emotional or spiritual wellbeing. This positive change can be achieved by something as simple as a smile, a kind gesture, a gentle touch, cooking someone a nice meal, helping them with a challenge, giving them a ride, sending healing energy or active listening. There are many people who are phenomenal healers who never recognize or acknowledge that they are indeed helping others and doing healing.

On a more formal level, there are many techniques and approaches to healing. Some healers focus on healing the physical body, while others focus on healing the mental, emotional and the spiritual body. Some techniques are very gentle and subtle, while others are more direct and can even be confrontational. I prefer gentle, direct approaches that quickly identify and clear the deepest root cause of a person's challenges. My methods dramatically raise an individual's soul frequency and vibration, and energetically clear and heal the entire person on all levels and dimensions of their being.

Because I am an empathic and I feel the pain, heartache and suffering of others, I have developed healing approaches that bypass the many layers of pain and suffering that people experience. This process allows me to almost instantly identify the deepest root cause of a person's challenges, often in a few minutes or less. Clearing at this level bypasses the many layers of trauma, and facilitates almost instantaneous healing and transformation. It is like sticking a pin in a balloon, or pulling out the bottom block in a tall stack of blocks. Once the core blockage is cleared, the person's entire mental, physical, emotional and spiritual energy structure positively realigns and heals.

Advanced intuitive healing creates multidimensional, high frequency, positive energy, awareness and consciousness, however it does not necessarily guarantee that a person's ailments will improve. In most cases, when a person's awareness and consciousness heal, their energy blockages dissolve and their physical body clears as well.

However, depending upon the individual's soul lessons and karma, their physical healing may or may not immediately happen. I have seen a few rare cases where there was a tremendous positive energetic shift with no obvious visible physical change or improvement. I have also witnessed massive energy releases in people who did not show any noticeable outward change physically, however their consciousness, personalities and energy field became noticeably lighter and happier.

In these rare cases, I felt that the person's soul, for whatever reason, had decided it was not the right time for the shift to happen on a physical level. I always do my absolute best to assist my clients to break free, but I am also well aware that everyone, along with their soul, guides and teachers, has infinite wisdom and the free will to choose to learn, change, grow and quickly heal — or not.

I readily admit that my desire to help people is very strong. However, over the years, I have learned to trust in the wisdom of a person's soul — and their chosen learning path — and not to be attached to achieving either the outcome the client said they wanted or the outcome I was wishing for them. I have also learned that people's actions speak a lot louder and truer than their words.

Whenever I experience a client who is in resistance or in denial, I verbally and energetically gently challenge their resistance three times. If I am not successful in breaking through their resistance, I back off and provide the best guidance and healing energy that I can offer, and that they are willing to accept at that given moment. I also make verbal and energetic suggestions, which I trust will expand their awareness and activate their commitment to their own healing process. When I do, I sincerely hope and desire for them to activate their consciousness and awaken their intention to learn, change, grow, shift and heal when they are ready. I respect their free will and the proper timing of their learning, changing, growing and healing.

Please note that just because a person is not open and receptive in this moment, does not mean that they will not be open and receptive in the next moment. When people are ready, they can change very quickly.

The Onion

Healing, therapy and personal transformation are often compared to working through the many layers of an onion. The goal is to get to the deepest core issue — the one throwing a person's physical body and energy field out of balance, and creating difficulties — and healing it. The onion analogy has been around for a long time and is considered by many people to be the way that traditional counseling, therapy and healing occurs. However, this model can represent a very long, slow process, as the practitioner helps the individual to peel away layer after layer of issues. This approach may take years or even decades to achieve — and, even after years of therapy, it may never uncover the core issue. This approach can take a tremendous amount of time, energy and can be very expensive.

If a practitioner lacks well-developed intuition, insight and they cannot read energy patterns, they have little choice other than to work through the client's issues, layer by layer, until they may or may not finally get to the core issue.

On the other hand, this entire process can often be accomplished in one session or one workshop by an intuitive energy healer who intuitively tracks energy and can access higher levels of consciousness, multi-dimensional realities, high frequency energy fields and their intuition. It also helps when the healer has extensive experience. When all of these factors are present — and when the client is open, willing and receptive — it is possible to identify the core issue and clear the blockage very quickly, many times in just one or a few sessions.

***

Bill, a man in his later thirties, was head Personal Development Trainer for a large, prestigious, multi-national firm to which I had been invited to give a presentation. Just before speaking to about 30 trainers and staff in that division, the Managing Director told me that I could only present and discuss my material — I was not allowed to touch or to work directly with anyone in the room.

About 15 minutes into my presentation, I stopped, looked at the entire personal development management group assembled in the room and apologized to them. I told them that I could not continue my presentation because without demonstrating my unique approach, they would not be able to comprehend what I was talking about. I said that my model for creating change and healing was so unique that it had to be taught by showing people what is possible, not by talking about it. The room fell so silent, I could have heard a pin drop.

After several very long uncomfortable moments, Bill, the head trainer who was sitting in the back of the room, stood up, stretched out his right arm and pointed his finger at me, and bravely shouted in front of all of his colleagues, "I do not know what you have, but I want it!"

After several more very uncomfortable moments of silence where everyone looked over at the senior management to see their reaction (which was to look down at the floor), I asked Bill to please come up to the front of the room. As he walked to the front, I instinctively walked towards the side of the room to give him space. This was not typical for me, as I usually stand right next to the person I am assisting.

I then asked Bill, "How may I serve you?"

Bill bravely answered, "I have been in counseling and therapy for over 13 years working on my mother issues and I just can't seem to crack it. What am I missing?"

After taking a few seconds to allow his question to settle, I intuitively sensed the answer he had been seeking for the past 13 years. Gently and with great compassion, I answered, "The reason you can't crack the issue with your mother is simple: the issue is not with your mother!"

I waited a little while to allow my words to sink in. Then I gave him the missing piece of the puzzle he had spent the past 13 years of his life searching for. I asked him, "Bill, did your father ever tell you that he loved you and respected you?"

Upon hearing this information, Bill instantly energetically and emotionally exploded. He broke down into hysterical crying and sobbed as if from the depths of his soul. A few minutes later, his crying subsided. As he regained his composure, everyone noticed that his appearance had dramatically changed. He looked much lighter, his aura became brighter, his energy field was stronger and was greatly expanded, and he seemed to have grown a few inches taller. Bill was finally free to be his true self! And all of this was the result of the single question I asked him!

I can only imagine how much time, energy and money Bill invested in his 13 years of counseling and therapy. I can only imagine the lifetime of stress, inner turmoil, pain and suffering he had experienced. Why had those other highly trained professionals not been able to see his core issue, which I intuitively saw immediately? I wonder how many other people have spent years or decades, seeking help without finding the answers, solutions or the healing they were seeking?

The speed and gentleness with which Bill's life was transformed doesn't have to be a rare incident. It is a normal everyday part of the healing and coaching sessions I offer.

As a result of Bill's breakthrough and the other breakthroughs achieved during my presentation, many of the organization's support staff, trainers and even senior managers requested personal session with me. I changed my travel plans, stayed much longer than I had planned to stay and worked extensively with most of the personal development team.

***

Jane came to see me because she was overweight, unhappy, lonely and wanted to find a partner. She was an Asian woman in her late thirties and as I listened to her, I was able to quickly identify her core issue. When I explained that she had been a twin in the womb and that her twin had died, she broke into hysterical crying. Then she shared her secret, asking me, "Is that why I always buy two of everything? Two identical irons, two identical pairs of shoes, two identical purses, two identical vacuum cleaners?" We then explored how that one traumatic incident had overshadowed her entire life and what positive changes she could make. One explanation was all it took!

Please note that very few of the people born who were twins in the womb are consciously aware of this. In most cases, even the parents are totally unaware that there had been a twin present. As I have said, about 20% of all single births were actually twins in the womb. Some were even triplets or more.

Intuition

Your intuition communicates to you through your physical body, your internal senses, your external senses and even through your dreams. It can operate on a basic level, such as survival instincts, however it can also be developed to assist you to see beyond all the illusions in life.

It is important to remember that your intuition is your connection to universal consciousness, which offers you direct access to all of the information in the universe from the beginning of time until the end of time. The level of intuition you have and the accuracy of your intuition depends to a large degree upon how much curiosity, openness, willingness, trust, faith and receptivity you have, and upon the amount of attention you pay to your senses.

Intuition is like a muscle or any other skill: the more you exercise, use it and practice, the stronger it becomes. As you clear and align your energy, your intuition communicates more clearly with you and is more precise. With practice, you gain greater access to more detailed information. Intuition can be taught; and everyone has access to this gift.

Intuition shouldn't be thought of as strange or unusual; it is simply an extension and expansion of our natural senses. There is no way that our ancestors would have survived — or that we'd be alive on this planet today — had it not been for their highly developed intuitive skills helping them to survive. Their highly developed intuition, combined with their natural senses, allowed humans to survive and thrive, even better than animals.

In the last few centuries, Western society moved away from favoring the sensing, feeling, right-brain, intuitive mind and has focused more on the left-brain, logical, thinking mind. As a result we have lost of lot of the gifts our intuition and right brain gave us.

The best of both worlds would include fully integrating a person's highly developed right-brain and their highly developed left-brain. When these work with each other in absolute balance and harmony, this would create a balanced whole-brain approach to everything we do. This blending of the left-brain masculine and right-brain feminine energy is referred to as the Whole Brain Approach and the Inner Marriage.

In ancient times, throughout all cultures, there were prophets, seers and healers. These highly gifted people were revered and extremely important to the survival of the native tribes. Even in the middle ages, there were many holistic practitioners.

Unfortunately, with the onset of The Black Plague, and the consolidation of power and control by organized religion during the middle ages, we have been indoctrinated into a more left-brain thinking process, and one controlled by science, Western medicine, the pharmaceutical companies and organized religious beliefs.

Ritual and Ceremony

Many of the ceremonies practiced in the past and some even today, were designed to help people to slow down, quiet their minds and to get in touch with their authentic feelings, emotions, senses and intuition. By design, many rituals and ceremonies are long, boring and repetitious, which automatically throws the conscious mind into an altered state. In an altered state, the conscious mind gets bored, stops thinking and analyzing, and relaxes its control. When that happens, it is more open and receptive to new ideas, energy and healing.

This is why most religious rituals are purposely long, repetitive and often boring, so that the conscious mind gets bored, gives up and stops thinking. It is one of the reasons why long drawn-out religious ceremonies can be so effective. The Native American

Vision Quest, pipe ceremonies, sweat lodges, sun dance and other very sacred spiritual ceremonies also incorporate these practices.

When expressed in a positive way, the principles used in rituals and ceremonies can be very positive and life affirming. However it is important to note that these exact same principles can be used in a manipulative way to break down people's defenses, implant negative thoughts and suggestions, and to control people.

Alcohol, mind-altering drugs, repetitious sounds, hypnotic music and subliminal messages can also be used to break down and break through the conscious mind. Advertising professionals know these principles and use them to manipulate us and motivate us to buy their products and services. Propaganda also taps into this principle to get us to believe and do things we would not normally agree with.

There are further dangers to this condition. When the conscious mind is too open and receptive, it loses its ability to think, analyze and protect us. When that happens, the mind's ability to discern between positive and negative suggestions and actions is weakened. This is one of the reasons why it is so important to always remain conscious of where you are, the people you associate with, what you are listening to and the choices you are making.

Although some people are comfortable listening to subliminal motivational and subliminal healing meditations, I am not. I choose to only listen to materials where I can hear, evaluate and choose whether the products are indeed positive, constructive and helpful, and discern whether they were made with the level of integrity I am committed to. For me, it is imperative that the languaging of the meditations, and in fact all communication, be positive and uplifting.

***

I've attended many Native American ceremonies where announcements were sent out telling people the time and location of the event. Very quickly, I learned that if the announcement said the ceremony would start at 11:00 a.m., most likely it would actually take place some time between 2:00 p.m. and 9:00 p.m. that evening. This is affectionately called "Indian Time."

I noticed an interesting change happen among the people who attended. People who were left-brained, concerned with time and control-oriented tended to get upset

*that the ceremony wasn't starting on time, and they would either leave or mellow.
By the time the ceremony started, those who had remained there had softened and
surrendered to the fact that the ceremony was going to start whenever it was going
to start — and not a moment sooner.*

This process of letting go, surrendering to what is happening, quieting the mind, being peaceful and being totally present in the moment is critical to being open and receptive to positive change. Using this approach, the Native American medicine people were preparing those attending to be more fully open, receptive and present to the sacredness and the potential benefits of the ceremony.

Drugs for Spiritual Advancement

Although some people believe that mind-altering drugs help to open the senses and increase awareness, intuition and healing abilities, I have found just the opposite to be true. In my experience, the senses and the spiritual gifts will open naturally as a person learns, changes, heals and evolves. Using drugs to increase a person's psychic powers and accelerate their spiritual growth could give the person a shorter and faster learning curve now, however there will usually be a price to pay later. I avoid taking drugs, even when I have been around other spiritual people who do.

***

*In 1987, I went to visit a spiritual group in Cottonwood, near Sedona,
Arizona, with an extremely psychic friend of mine who is one of the best spiritual
trans-channels I have ever met. As we walked towards the building, we noticed a
number of people in the distance, standing outside the building. All of a sudden,
my friend exploded emotionally and very uncharacteristically started shouting to
me, "These people do not have any idea what they are doing! They are taking
drugs to speed their spiritual growth, however, it will take them lifetimes to repair
the damage — the holes — these drugs are creating in their auras and energy
fields! What are these people thinking! What are these people doing to
themselves?"*

*Her observation and reaction says it all. We all have choices and with our
choices always come consequences. Although the spiritual teacher of this group
probably meant well when he encouraged his followers to take the mind-altering*

drugs to expand their awareness and open their spiritual centers, the group members were unknowingly risking severe consequences. One of the most important lessons for everyone on the spiritual path is to use extreme discernment whenever we are asked to give our power away to other people, especially to those we choose as our spiritual teachers.

Addictions

Addictions can involve a wide range of chemicals, drugs, habits and behaviors. They include addictions to sugar, coffee, power, recreational and prescription drugs, alcohol, sex, money, love, television, computer games, mobile phones, digital devices and many more. A person can also be addicted to anger, depression and abuse. There are other types of addictions, which on the surface may appear healthy, such as extreme sports, dieting and exercise, which can be harmful if done in excess. When we are addicted to something, we give up our power and control; the habit or the substance is in control of us. It is important that we live in balance and are in control of our lives. Any time we give up our power and control over our thoughts, actions or our life, we are being dysfunctional.

***

John, an English man in his early 20's, phoned me because he was hooked on hard drugs and alcohol. He was scared and wanted to have a session with me as soon as possible.

When I asked him if he was still using, he said that he was. Normally I don't see or work with anyone who is still actively using. But as I talked to John, my intuition clearly gave me the message that even though he was still using, I was supposed to see him and help him. Despite the fact that it was after 9:00 p.m. at night when he called, he wanted to come over and for me to do his session immediately. I told him the first time I could see him was in a few days. He asked what the earliest appointment that day was and I said 9 a.m. On the day of the appointment, even though it was only 9 a.m., he arrived drunk and on drugs — and he was driving.

Once again, I started to tell John that I couldn't work with him until he stopped using, however my intuition once again instructed me to work with him anyway. As we began the session, I received a strong intuitive message that he had to come off all the drugs and alcohol cold turkey — all at once. When I conveyed this message to John, he told me that his doctor told him that if he came off all of the drugs and alcohol at once, it could kill him.

Again I went deep inside to ask my intuition for guidance and again I was told that he had to come off everything all at once. I then made it perfectly clear to John that I was not a doctor and could not advise him from a medical perspective. Only his doctor could do that. I told him that he had to make his own decision regarding the approach he wanted to take and I made it perfectly clear that whatever he chose to do was fine with me.

John decided to continue and complete his session, however he did not contact me for any further follow-up sessions. A few weeks after his session, I started receiving phone calls from people I had never met who were John's close friends. They asked what I had done to John. As I had not seen or heard from him since that one session, I had no clue what was going on and I asked how he was doing. They told me that John was totally clear of his drug and alcohol addiction and was doing amazingly well.

Over a year later, I was giving a talk in London when a man came up to me and said hello. He asked if I remembered him and I told him I didn't. He explained that he was John, the man who had been hooked on drugs and alcohol when he came to see me. He thanked me, we shook hands and he sat down in the audience. Later in the presentation, I invited John to come up on stage and share his story, which he did and everyone gave him a heartfelt round of applause.

A week later I again started getting phone calls from John's friends, once again asking what I had done to him. Not having a clue, I asked why they were calling me. They said that John was furious with me, that he had a total relapse, and was back on drugs and alcohol.

A few days later I called John and asked how he was doing and what was going on. What he said was probably one of the most stunning words I have ever heard. He said, "At the talk I found out that you are only human. I thought you were a God who had waved a magic wand over my head and cured me. I don't think I'm strong enough to heal myself."

I made it very clear to John that he had taken responsibility and changed his life around. All I did was to help guide and support him by clearing and aligning his energy field; he had done all the rest. Regardless of what I said, John insisted that he was not wise enough, strong enough or capable enough to remain clean and sober on his own. After that call, I lost touch with John.

This is a great example of a person with a negative self-image and low self-esteem who refused to believe that he was capable, on his own, of taking responsibility and being healed. John just could not imagine that he had the courage, strength, power and commitment to break free — even though he had already achieved it for an entire year — so after a year of being clean and sober, he went back on drugs and alcohol. This story is extremely sad. Unfortunately, it is completely true.

* * *

12-Step Recovery Programs

Twelve-step recovery programs — as well as treatment programs for anger, codependency, substance abuse and Post Traumatic Stress Disorder (PTSD) — have helped millions of people worldwide.

With all my 12-step clients, I add three additional processes that can greatly improve both the short and long-term benefits from these programs.

In the first process, I scan the person's energy field and energy levels. This quickly pinpoints the root cause of what is undermining and throwing their energy out of balance — thereby causing, creating, allowing and amplifying both their behavior and addictions. The second process is to clear their energy field of all negative discordant energies. The third process is to realign their energy with their pure soul essence.

Regardless of the person's addictions or recovery challenges, adding these three processes can greatly accelerate, as well as ease their recovery process — and would also minimize the danger of them relapsing.

When a person is ready, fully committed and willing to take personal responsibility, these three processes can be achieved in a single healing session.

The Issue of Dimensions

Imagine a vertical ladder with an infinite number of steps. Now imagine that each rung represents a different and separate dimensional reality. Starting at the bottom, with each step upwards on this ladder there is an increase in the dimensional reality and a corresponding increase in the energy, frequency, vibration, consciousness and complexity. Each dimension has its own set of rules, universal laws and characteristics.

The Earth has long functioned as a third-dimensional place of learning; however it is currently in transition as it shifts to a higher fourth-dimensional frequency and vibration. Some beings here can now consciously access and function at these higher frequencies, vibrations and dimensions, while others are still operating at lower frequencies.

People operating at lower third dimensional energy frequencies are more focused on themselves and operate more from a time-based, materialistic, ego-personality level. These people are more focused on getting their personal wants, needs and desires satisfied. They tend to shirk responsibility, be highly competitive and combative, or they are lazy and blame others for their misfortune. They think short term, and want their gratification and rewards now. Often these people are fear based and tend to think they are right, and that their race, religion and approach to everything is the right way, and the only way. Often they cannot and will not, see or accept the viewpoints, values, rights and choices of others. These people are exclusive, not inclusive. They have many prejudices and tend to cling to older more conservative, even rigid, black and white forms of attitudes, beliefs, structures, values and realities.

The people operating on higher dimensions have more concern for the overall good of all individuals, including their community, the environment, all of life and the world. They are more sensitive, caring, open, receptive, loving and inclusive. They tend to take personal responsibility for their actions and will do their best to peacefully communicate, negotiate and ask for what they desire. They embrace diversity and put the needs of their community, country and the world above their personal desires. They are willing to delay their gratification and tend to think about the long-term consequences of their actions. These people, who are committed to the greater good, tend to make the best workers, teachers and leaders.

Healing, coaching, mentoring and doing readings at the third dimensional level can provide a client with useful information. However, those of us who operate at higher levels of consciousness can go far beyond this. We can read energy patterns, tap into our intuition and access higher dimensional realities. By doing this we can facilitate profound life-changing healings, bring forth greater insights into current and future possibilities, resolve relationship challenges and assist in the creation of prosperity. We can clearly see the solutions to current challenges, as well as future potentials and possibilities that are not obvious at the third dimensional level. Another advantage is that this overall process is much faster.

Past Lives: Answers From The Past

The topic of past lives has long been interesting and highly debated. I have witnessed many occasions where the answers and solutions to a client's challenges did not seem to exist in this lifetime. The challenge itself — whether it pertained to prosperity, health, pain, suffering, illness, disease, relationships, self-sabotage or anything else — could be energetically tracked back through time and space to a specific decision the person made about life and living — or to an event where the energy became blocked. Because time operates within a continuum, everything can be tracked back to the source regardless of whether it occurred in this lifetime or in another lifetime. On numerous occasions, as I was intuitively tracking the energy of a client's challenge, I was led to other lifetimes and places. When this happened, I'd get pictures, images, feelings and knowings that provided the key information that led me to the client's breakthrough.

Whether or not these insights came from an actual past life or whether they came from genetic history, cellular memory or even from a good story doesn't really matter. What matters is that tracking the energy to its source is tremendously fast, effective and yields tangible positive results.

***

When the subject of past lives comes up, I often jokingly say, "Don't worry if you don't believe in past lives this lifetime, you will next lifetime!"

***

When I was in Alaska, I met John, a man in his early 40s, who complained that his leg hurt every time he was near the ocean. When he was further inland, his leg was fine. This confused and made no sense to him. One day, as I was driving on a very bumpy back dirt road with John, I got a crystal clear past-life image in my mind of him standing at the bow of a whaling skiff with a harpoon in his right hand. Attached to the harpoon was a long rope, which was coiled in a low half barrel on the floor of the skiff. As John threw the harpoon it struck his target, a whale or large walrus, penetrating it. The animal dove deep and the line attached to the harpoon went flying out of the boat into the water. Unfortunately for John, his leg got caught in the harpoon line. He was dragged overboard and drowned. When I shared what I had seen with John, the pain instantly disappeared and never returned.

In many cases, once a past life trauma is explained and understood, the residual pain melts away, never to return. Using an intuitive energy tracking process, I have assisted countless people to release many kinds of fears: fear of being in the water (drowning), fear of flying, fear of knives and fear of intimacy. Almost all unexplained fears have their roots in genetic history, energetic attachments or unresolved past lifetime trauma.

***

One day while walking with some friends in the vicinity of Bell Rock, in Sedona, Arizona, I suddenly felt an overwhelming sadness come over me that I didn't understand. It was as if I dropped into an emotional black hole. I called to my friends who I was walking with and we tuned into the energies together.

Apparently, in another lifetime I was an old Native American man who was too old and slow to keep up and travel with my group. As was the custom in those days, my clan sat me under a shade tree with some food and water, and after making sure I was comfortable, they continued on, leaving me to die. In that lifetime, I had died on that very spot.

Once we received this information, I took some quality time to acknowledge my love and respect for the people I had traveled with in that lifetime. As I did this, I felt the sadness that had overcome me slowly melt away.

Perspective: Heaven, Nirvana and Paradise vs. Hunker Down

A number of the major Earth religions teach that if you follow their teachings and rules, do good deeds, sacrifice yourself and quietly suffer your fate on Earth, you will reap great rewards in Heaven. They speak of life after death and especially of heaven, nirvana, paradise and the Afterlife, as being far better than and preferable to your life on Earth. The promise of the reward of everlasting joy, happiness and streets paved with gold does sound inviting.

Unfortunately, this perspective often sets people up to live a life of mental, emotional, physical and even spiritual submission, to the religions doctrines and the religious leaders. This sets people up to be fearful of being fully energetically present in their physical body, of living life fully, and of fully participating in and fully enjoying the human Earth experience. This concept brings with it the fear of making a mistake, because if they do, they might not go to these wonderful places when they die. As a result, people who see life this way tend to avoid the risk of being fully alive, passionate about life, risking and being fully present in their physical Earth body.

This perspective can also bring up other fears as well, including the fear of enjoying the human experience too much, and the fear of becoming too attached to and trapped in the Earth energy due to enjoying it so much. Other fears come up around making mistakes, fully living and enjoying the Earth experience, and knowingly or unknowingly going against the teachings of organized religion. Some religions, especially in the past, have even used the threat of excommunication and going to hell as a way to scare and control people. All of these fear-based teachings set up the polarity of hope in the "Rewards in Heaven" and a fear of "Punishment in Hell."

This message can be wrongly interpreted to mean that by committing suicide, a person can avoid and escape their learning process, and go directly to Paradise. As discussed earlier, when people commit suicide, they have to come back to Earth again, face the issues they avoided and complete their learning their lessons — sometimes with even more challenges added on to their plate.

Some native cultures like the Hawaiians and the Maoris of New Zealand embrace the philosophy of "hunkering down" that refers to becoming 100% present and completely grounded in your physical body. They believe in fully embracing the Earth plane experience. In truth, being fully present can help you to stay grounded and connected, and that supports you in learning your lessons more quickly. Although these cultures are spiritually-oriented, their focus is on fully living this life rather than making an Afterlife preferable to and more sacred than life on Earth.

Dominance Over vs. Respect For Nature

I find it interesting that some religions and cultures honor and respect the Earth as our mother and provider, while other religions and cultures seem to have little or no respect for nature, animals, plants or Mother Earth. Some religions and cultures consider humans to be far superior to the rest of creation, and seem to teach that it is acceptable to pillage, rape and destroy the resources of our planet.

Yet, most indigenous tribes and cultures, which many educated people consider to be primitive and heathen, respect all of creation, as being our brothers and sisters — as being our equals — and respect all life, including all plants, animals, fish, birds, insects, trees, water, mountains and the entire Earth. They learned in ancient times that if they did not honor, respect and take care of the Earth, they would destroy the very environment that supported them.

The indigenous people learned to live in harmony with their environment and have deep respect, even reverence, for all of creation. They knew that humans were just a small part of a much bigger ecosystem.

When will our "advanced" materialistic consumer society recognize what seems so obvious?

Religion and Spirituality

I believe that few, if any, of the world's religious leaders of the past ever wanted to or intended to start a world religion. Most were just sharing their truths and hoping that others would benefit. Devotees and followers often started these religions many years after the death of their particular beloved teacher, without truly knowing or understanding what the teacher really knew.

Religion, as a whole, does its best to provide explanations, structure and values to help people deal with the everyday challenges, chaos and confusion of life. Frequently it offers a set of values to help and guide people. It also does its best to explain how life got started, how it evolved and how to be a good person. Unfortunately, many religions are old, fear-based (rather than love-based), patriarchal models that have failed to keep pace with the changing times and the needs of people.

Most religions seem to be part of something so much bigger and more expansive, yet different religions fail to respect each other and work together for the common good of all people. In fact, since the beginning of time, much of the fighting and killing on planet Earth has been done in the name of religion, where one religion considers itself to be right/good and considers another religion to be wrong/evil. Hence, they attempt to compete with, convert, kill and destroy each other. Because of these outdated attitudes, most organized religions are losing members rapidly.

Spirituality is based on many profound things: universal truths, traditions that go back many thousands of years, practices of honoring the Earth and natural laws that can be demonstrated. Spirituality goes far beyond organized religion, although most religions include many spiritual teachings. Spirituality is about having a direct and personal relationship with God/Spirit, without having to go through or be controlled by intermediaries.

In almost all organized religions, people are taught and conditioned to consider their religious leaders as the only ones who possess the knowledge and know the pathway to divine truth. Religions also depend on the assessments, donations and tithing of people in order to maintain their buildings and their lifestyle. Few religions are willing to tell people that they, as individuals, already have within them the ability to connect directly to the Source.

During much of history, men had only three ways available to them to make a living: agriculture/farming, fighting/military and religion. Most of the religious doctrines and dogma have been rewritten from their original texts to instill fear and to create a sense of dependency in the people, so the religious leaders could maintain dominance and control over them.

Many religious and spiritual leaders have kept a lot of spiritual truths and advanced information hidden from the masses. Some leaders felt that knowing the truth was too dangerous for the masses, while other religious leaders felt that they would lose their control if ordinary people knew the truth.

What was taught to the general public was very different from the knowledge that was kept secret by the Christian Church, the Jewish Kabala and the Mystery Schools of Egypt. Many secret societies around the world still hold on to some very powerful truths, healing skills and powerful methods of manifestation, yet they do not share this with the masses.

You must choose what you want to believe and the path you wish to follow. For me, I have chosen the spiritual path as opposed to a strict religious one. At the same time, I can see the good that some aspects of organized religion provide.

Shakespeare

Shakespeare said, "All the world is a stage and all men and women merely players." So it is: from a divine perspective, we are all actors and actresses playing out our parts. It is time to do this more kindly, gently, compassionately and with more conscious awareness. It is also important to note that we have free will, and we can go backstage and change our costumes, the part we play and how we play it, anytime we wish.

The Buddha on Reaching Enlightenment

It is said that the Buddha spiritually blossomed and reached enlightenment by sitting under the Bodhi Tree, staying totally present, suspending all judgment and allowing himself to fully embrace, feel and become many of the polarities of Earth. He became the polarities of the murderer and the murdered. He embraced and became the polarities of the rapist and the raped, as well as the thief and the victim. It is this process of staying totally present, of letting go of all judgment, including self-judgment and accepting what is that allows us to dramatically accelerate our soul growth.

When we let go of all of our judgments about right and wrong, good and bad, then we enter into a space of greater love and compassion. It is in this place, where we experience more love, faith, trust and peace. When we accept people as they are, without trying to change them, control them or get love from them, then we spiritually open and blossom. Our soul growth is accelerated, when we choose to love, honor, respect, trust, have faith and accept ourselves — and others.

Fully living in the perfection of the moment is all we can hope for, while at the same time always doing the best we can to stay conscious and do good.

Objectivity and Perspective
For Healing Oneself

There are proverbs in both the legal and medical fields that make a lot of sense: "A person who represents himself in court has a food for a client." This is also true for someone seeking medical attention. The reason for this is that seldom can someone remain objective about a situation or see their issues clearly, when it is about themselves or about people close to them.

It is important for all of us, including world-class healers, to maintain close associations and connections with other world-class healers, intuitives and energy medicine experts around the planet so we continue to receive the guidance, help, support and healing we need in order to keep learning, changing and growing.

We all need healing, guidance and support, and we are all on a journey. Some of us are further ahead in one area, while others are further ahead in other areas. It is the team, the group, the collaboration and the synergy that makes us strong, and allows us to do the teaching and the real challenging healings.

Much of what I have learned over my lifetime was gleamed from other healers, shamans and medicine people I have met and shared healing experiences with. Other spiritual information has come to me through conscious, unconscious and even dream state remembering. Often as I watch another healer, regardless of their approach, I remember past lives where I also used that approach. This remembering allows me to also reclaim that skill.

Please know that we are never alone. Whenever I am communicating with a client or doing healing work, I am constantly accessing my intuition, higher realms of consciousness, and communicating with my guides, teachers and helpers — and those of my client — to gain the most information possible so I can assist my client.

There is a huge difference between a person who gives his power and responsibility away to others, and asks others to "fix him." As opposed to someone who takes full responsibility for their life and their actions, and seeks further knowledge, advice and healing so that he can continue to learn, change and grow.

I repeat, "Only a fool represents (or treats) himself or his loved ones, as a client (or patient)!" If I had not sought out and received the guidance, assistance and healing from the many shamans, healers and medicine people I met along the path, I would not be at the level where I am today. Please be open and receptive to being helped, healed and supported!

Although I consider myself to be spiritual, rather than religious, I do like the statement, "Where two or more are gathered in my name (Spirit), there I am with them!"

Chapter 11
Near-Death, Death and Reincarnation

The Near-Death Experience

Near-death experiences (NDE) happen when people energetically leave their physical bodies and find themselves in a place where they can choose between dying or staying on Earth — and they choose to stay. An NDE can be triggered by a severe shock, trauma, bad accident, high fever, serious illness, surgery, or other unexpected situations. As our society begins to acknowledge these experiences, more and more people are coming forward to describe their experiences of choosing life or death. Most people who had NDE's describe feeling great awareness, peace, harmony, love, compassion, respect and support when they reach the other side. No one has ever reported being scared, criticized, judged or threatened with being sent to hell.

Almost every person who's had an NDE reports being met by wise, loving divine beings, as well as by close family, friends and loved ones who have passed on. Their experiences sound like heartfelt reunions and celebrations; most people who have had a near-death experience do not want to come back from the profound love, peace, joy and harmony they feel on the other side.

It's very interesting that people are usually welcomed into their NDE experience — this place of bright white light, great peace and tranquility — only by beings fitting in with their personal earthly belief systems and religious preferences. They are met with scenes and situations that they are comfortable and familiar with on Earth.

For example, a Christian might be welcomed and greeted by Jesus, and most likely would not be met by Buddha, Krishna or other deities that they have no connection with this lifetime.

People who have had these experiences and have chosen to return to their life on Earth tend to be positively changed by their experience. Most have lost their fear of death and dying. They are calmer, more relaxed and have lost their sense of urgency in life. They enjoy the present moment more and are more at peace with themselves, the people around them and their life circumstances.

End of Lifetime

Upon death, our souls energetically disconnect from our physical body and we take with us all of the wisdom, knowledge, learnings and skills we gained while we experienced life on the Earth plane. We cannot and do not take with us any material wealth.

Many people who have had a near-death experience (NDE) report traveling through a tunnel with bright white light at the other end. They frequently report seeing their loved ones, who had previously passed on, joyfully waiting to greet them on the other side. Within the tunnel there is a *"point of no return"* where the person intuitively sensed that past that point, there is no coming back. But prior to passing that point, they could choose to return to life.

Not one person I know or have read about has ever reported any sign of a Heaven or Hell, except for the images people created while they were alive on Earth. Many report that dying and death are like falling asleep at night and waking up on *"the other side"* without their physical body and without any pain, suffering or limitations.

When the soul arrives on the other side, it rests for a while, healing and releasing any trauma it experienced on Earth. After healing and adjusting to the energy on the other side, there is an *"after life"* review where the soul meets with a team of advanced beings who help review what that soul learned, what was done well and where additional learning is still needed.

The team, with the soul's input, determines what the next growth step will be for the soul. After a rest, recovery and an integration period, the soul is ready to make the choice either to return to the Earth plane or to go someplace else for further learning. There is always guidance, healing and support available to assist in making this choice.

***

Sandra, a very spiritual Australian woman in her mid 60's, was bitten by a highly poisonous spider while visiting the USA and went into a coma. For five days, she was on the edge between life and death, and had many visions. As she faced her decision about whether to remain on Earth or to die and go into spirit, she became aware of three relationships in her life where she didn't feel she could say, "Well Done!" Realizing this, she made the decision to remain alive on Earth and clear up these three unresolved situations.

Note: Staying alive was definitely the best option for Sandra, however she could have chosen to leave the planet and resolve these relationships in another lifetime. We are always at choice, and it is always best to resolve as much as we possibly can in our present lifetime.

***

Elaine, a European woman in her late 30s described what happened to her when her father died. She was in the middle of a conversation with her boyfriend when she suddenly blacked out and became unconscious. Her scared boyfriend kept shaking her and even slapped her to try to get her to wake up. Nothing had any effect. She remained unconscious.

Elaine described the event in detail from her perspective. Her father, who had been living over two thousand miles away from her, had just died of cancer. Immediately upon his death, he energetically came in his spirit form looking for her, wanting her to transition with him. He felt lonely and was scared, and did not want to be alone or to go into the spirit world alone. Elaine described her father pulling her through a tunnel of light, which extended from the Earth dimension to the spiritual planes. As they reached the point of no return — the point at which there was no going back to Earth for Elaine — she heard her two children frantically screaming and calling her name, begging her to please come back.

She was torn between going with her father and the frantic cries of her children. Her children's voices were so strong that she finally looked at her father and told him that she couldn't go with him, because she needed to stay and take care of her children. She told him that he needed to go on by himself and she watched him move on alone past the point of no return. Instantly, everything changed as the scene before her began to fade away and she started to regain consciousness.

Elaine and her boyfriend were both quite shaken up by the experience. Within minutes of regaining consciousness, she called me and asked me to help her to understand what had just happened. As I explained her experience to her in spiritual terms that she could understand and accept, she was able to relax and feel more peaceful.

The Death and Dying Process

From a spiritual perspective, it is not important whether a fetus, child or adult lives for only a few seconds or until they are over 100 years old. The age at which a person dies does not indicate the value, success, lessons or wisdom that the soul accumulates. Some souls only need to be on Earth for a very short time. Others are called away by circumstances or are needed in other locations in the Universe. Sometimes souls come in primarily to teach their parents lessons, while at other times souls come in to teach medical doctors or the world a lesson.

As parents, we always wish the best for our children and we want our children to outlive us, however we have to understand that the destiny of all human beings is completely up to their soul and their Higher Self. Highly skilled therapists have reported being in the middle of deep hypnosis sessions with a client when a spiritual voice very clearly said, "Stop your sessions immediately! If you continue to try to help this person, there will no longer be a reason for them to be alive and we will be forced to terminate their life."

Although losing a loved one is challenging, especially when it is our own children or close loved ones, we must learn to let go of our preconceptions of life and death, and trust the wisdom of each soul and the greater wisdom of the universe.

People who have had a near death experience during a medical operation or accident often describe experiences of floating outside or above their body. They report having been able to see the entire scene below them in great detail and they could clearly hear everything that everyone present was saying and even thinking.

They frequently describe being met by loved ones, guides and teachers who communicate with them and are waiting to assist them. Some people are given a choice as to whether to stay alive on Earth and learn more, or to move on into spirit and leave this lifetime. If we leave this lifetime without learning and completing our lessons, we will have to come back again and again and again until we complete the learning lesson. Please remember that living and being alive on Earth is not a punishment — it is a gift and an honor. We, as souls, are the ones choosing to be here.

The Death Process

Most of us go to sleep and trust that we will wake up the next morning. As we go to sleep, most of us have very little fear or anxiety about falling asleep. During our sleeping hours, we are not consciously aware that we are sleeping, unless we are dreaming. In many ways, the process of dying is very similar to going to sleep at night.

The death process is one of shedding our physical form and moving on into spirit, which is our energy body. The transition is neither traumatic nor painful. When a person is conscious and at peace with their death and dying process, it can be very easy and painless, just like going to sleep at night and waking up the next morning. Except in this case, the person wakes up in another reality.

Unfortunately, what many of us have been taught and conditioned to think about death can make things more challenging for us than they need to be. If you have been indoctrinated to believe that you are going to be judged and punished for everything you have ever done wrong and every mistake you have made this lifetime, it is easy to be fearful of dying and facing this judgment. This is especially true if you have been taught to believe in heaven and hell.

Personally, I do not believe in heaven or hell; I only believe that we should do our best in each and every moment. Everyone makes mistakes. Everyone has lied, cheated, been dishonest and has hurt someone at some point in their life. Hopefully, we all learn, change, grow and become wiser as we progress in life and grow older. It is important for each of us to do our best to make amends and to create peace. It is extremely helpful to remember that the most important person to forgive and to make peace with is ourselves.

Unlike our generation, previous generations have accepted and embraced the sacred initiation of dying and death. In the past, the body of a deceased family member was cleansed and prepared at home by their loved ones, and then kept at home until the time of burial. Nowadays, we distance ourselves from death and have others do these things for us. By doing so, we separate ourselves from the opportunity of being an active part of the death and dying process. This is also true with the birthing process.

For those of us losing a loved one, it is important to fully feel and release our feelings and emotions around loss. This can be achieved by letting all of our feelings and emotions out, either by talking to the dying person or by creating a ritual to say goodbye, either before or after the person has passed. Other life experiences can be as traumatic or even more traumatic than losing a loved one, such as moving, leaving a person or the loss of a pet. It is very important to fully embrace and release these natural and normal emotions as much as possible, and to have closure about the situation. If you don't, it can affect your ability to be open to intimacy and love in the future.

In some cultures, when a child is born, the tribe or clan will cry and express sorrow because the person has entered the Earth experience. In other cultures, people do just the opposite and rejoice when a child is born. The same is true for death: some cultures celebrate it and express joy at someone's death, while other cultures express mostly sadness and grief. This is all about perspective and beliefs.

***

In early November of 2017, I learned that my cousin Stanley's health was rapidly deteriorating. Stan had been like an older brother and a good friend to me. He was the only family member who had kept in touch with me, and had been there for me when I needed help and support this lifetime. During the past few years we talked on the phone almost every week.

Stan was 86 years old and had been in good health, however now his health was declining rapidly. His wife kept me informed of the state of his decline and made airline reservations for me to fly in to be with him.

On Sunday, November 19th, I suddenly felt an urgency to immediately get on a plane and fly out to see him. I changed the flight dates, flew out the next day and was fortunate to spend the last three days of Stan's life with him.

Although he never regained consciousness and I was never able to "verbally" talk with him or him with me, I was able to hold his hand and to talk to him from my heart to his heart.

As his friends and family do not believe spiritually as I do, I quietly mentally talked with him, shared what I knew about the death, dying and transition process, said sacred prayers, called in his departed loved ones to assist him in his transition, and I kept clearing his energy field of fear, pain and trauma.

This was a very profound experience for me, for although I had lost many loved ones and been to many funerals, this was the first time that I had the privilege of sitting with a loved one as they transitioned.

During those last three days, I spent many hours sitting by my cousin's side, holding his hand, clearing his energy field and talking with him mind-to-mind. I was sitting with him touching his arm as he took his last breath — and for a few hours afterwards.

This was not a scary process, although it was one that I had never experienced in this lifetime. It was honoring, peaceful and respectful. I share this because it is so important to be able to be totally present with a person, especially a loved one, as they transition.

My sole, and soul, purpose for flying out to be with my cousin and his wife during his transition was to support both of them in this sacred process.

Please, whenever a person is approaching the end of their life, reach out to them, tell them all the good things and all the good times you remember, tell them all that they have done right and thank them for the many ways they enriched your life.

This is not a time for negativity, being angry, lashing out or for punishing a person. It is a time for great forgiveness, compassion and humility.

Heaven and Hell

One of the many interesting concepts on Earth is that of heaven and hell. While we may never know who created this concept and the reason it was created, it has influenced and affected many people over thousands of years.

Some religious groups describe heaven and hell as real physical places. To date, neither humans nor science have been able to prove that such places actually exist. Nor can they identify the location of these mythical locales.

Heaven is described as a place where people gain entry or are sent after they die as a reward for good behavior, including living a pious life filled with good deeds. Some religions promise that when a person sacrifices, dedicates themselves to the rules of the religion and lives in service to others, they will reap great rewards in heaven. Some religions also claim that if a person suffers greatly while alive, they will somehow be granted extra bonus points in heaven when they die. This delayed gratification is part of the theme of aggrandizing and encouraging acts of loyalty, self-sacrifice, being a victim and being a martyr. The concept of heaven is presented (marketed) as a place where "good" people lead an idyllic eternal life of joy, happiness, health, abundance, ease, grace and great wealth.

On the other hand, we are told that hell is a place where people are sent when they do not follow the doctrine of the church or other organized religion, do bad deeds, are selfish, self-centered or take advantage of other people. This includes people who lie, steal, cheat and kill. Hell is described as a place of intense pain and eternal suffering. This concept of judgment, eternal punishment, suffering and pain is meant to put the fear of God or of making a mistake in people.

Most Eastern religions believe in the Law of Karma, which claims, "What you sow, so shall you reap." This means that what you do to others and especially to yourself, comes back to you. So if you live a good life and treat others and yourself with respect, kindness and decency, then good comes back to you and you move in a positive spiritual direction. If you harm others or yourself, by lying, stealing, killing or acting in ways that are less than ethical and moral, then similar bad things come back to you and you move in a negative spiritual direction.

It is important to note that on a soul level, acts of subservience — including giving up one's personal power and inner knowing to follow a set of rules and the dictates of others — can be self-defeating and can create negative karma. Only when a person sees the error of their ways and changes, reclaiming their sacred power and inner-knowing, does the energy neutralize and switch to the positive.

Although some religions talk about heaven and hell, and even describe it in detail, there is no proof it actually exists. From a scientific and energetic point of view there is no basis for the existence of an actual heaven or hell.

The only place I have been able to find heaven or hell has been right here on Earth. A person who is true to their soul essence, who moves forward in harmony with universal laws, loves, honors, respects and supports themselves and others, tends to lead a life of peace, joy and happiness. This is as close to heaven as one can get here on Earth. Those people who don't do these things will experience pain and suffering — thereby creating their own living hell.

From everything I have learned and experienced, I believe there is no one outside of ourselves judging us; we are the only ones standing in judgment of ourselves. The human experience is about learning, changing, growing and expanding our consciousness. In this process, it is natural and normal for us to be tempted and to make mistakes. Moreover, when you are open and receptive to learning from your mistakes and to making positive course corrections regarding your thoughts, attitudes, beliefs and behaviors, you make progress and your soul frequency increases. However, if you do not learn from previous mistakes and keep repeating the same mistakes over and over again, you'll attract negative energy and your soul frequency decreases.

The duality concepts of heaven and hell, reward and punishment, carrot and stick, are scare tactics designed to threaten, brainwash and control people. In many cases, the original religious teachings, which were pure and loving, were rewritten to benefit the religions or political groups dictating the rules. It's interesting that some actions and behaviors that are considered bad in one religion or society are not necessarily wrongful or sinful in another religion or society. Religious and social rules, and doctrines in different countries can greatly disagree and even completely contradict each other.

Many religions organizations and governments do not trust people to be true to their divine nature, or to have the inner ethics and the moral strength to make the right decisions for themselves. For these reasons, they created laws, rules and regulations with penalties that punish unacceptable behavior. If people lived their divine expression and their highest truth, society would have no need for rules and laws because everyone would be guided by their own internal sense of right and wrong.

Taking absolute responsibility for your thoughts, actions and deeds is the best path forward. Doing your best to be kind, fair, honest, considerate and to live in integrity with yourself and others, is the key to living a good life.

(Note: The word "sin" originates from an old Jewish and Greek term meaning failure or missing the mark. So try again and do better next time. This is similar to saying that you have made an error: please keep practicing until you get it right.)

Reincarnation and Religion

In the Far East, reincarnation has been taught for many thousands of years and is a strong part of their culture and religion. *Reincarnation* is defined as the recurring cycle of birth, death and rebirth. It is a continuous cycle that can include hundreds or many thousands of lifetimes on Earth. The purpose of reincarnation is to offer an individual the opportunity to learn, change, grow, test themselves and gain wisdom from their Earthly experiences.

Most of the gurus and master teachers are aware of the Universal Laws and spiritual principles, one of which is reincarnation. It is interesting to note that many religions around the world started out teaching reincarnation as part of their religion; only it was later decided by subsequent leaders to take these teachings out of the information provided to the public, and to only share these with their inner circle or more advanced disciples.

***

When I travelled to Israel for three months in 1995 and met Hasidic, Ultraorthodox Jewish people, I was concerned about bringing up topics that might offend them. To my amazement, when I finally asked if they believed in reincarnation, beings of light and other spiritual subjects, they said, "Of course we do."

As I became more confident and asked more questions, they laughed at me and told me that many sacred teachings are only shared with those who have studied extensively. The mystical side of Judaism is called Kabbalah. Its teachings are not shared with the general public.

Over the years, I have learned that all religions — the Christian church, Native Americans and every other religious group I have studied with — keep their most sacred teachings and truths secret. Only their innermost circle knows the truth about the founders, the original teachings and the inner workings of the religion. In most cases, the true teachings have been kept from the general public.

The Gnostics — the original followers of Jesus — and others who Jesus taught believed wholeheartedly in the principles of reincarnation and other spiritual principles. Unfortunately, the vast majority of Jesus' teachings have been reinterpreted, retranslated, rewritten and watered down by people who inserted their own prejudices and agendas into the texts. I wonder how Jesus and other spiritual teachers would feel about the way their teachings and religions are being taught at this time, if they came back to Earth today.

We human beings have a way of interpreting things according to our own limited understanding, as well as our own wants, needs, thoughts, attitudes, beliefs, fears, prejudices and agendas. As Christianity and other religions evolved, the original teachings were changed, diluted and modified to fit the agendas of those rewriting history.

Many of the original devout Christian sects, including the Gnostics, were hunted down and killed because they knew the truth and were a threat to those who were modifying Jesus' teachings.

Then the Council of 312 A.D. got together and reviewed all the teachings and scriptures, selecting only what they wanted to keep and discarded the rest. They also modified, rewrote and reinterpreted what was written to suit their own agenda.

The primary reason the topic of reincarnation was taken out of many religious teachings was because religious leaders feared that if people knew that they had more than one lifetime to learn their lessons, they would not let themselves be so controlled by those in power. So instead of teaching the people the truth and trusting them to evolve in a positive manner, those in command created the concepts of heaven and hell to control people and scare them into submission.

In all cultures and countries around the globe, the victor always rewrites history according to what they believe and what they want people to know. Seldom is what is written about purely factual; it usually contains only what the conqueror, those in power, wants to present to history.

When Europeans invaded what is now America, Central America and South America, The Native Americans, Aztec, Mayan and many other cultures were far more spiritually connected and far more advanced in many ways — even scientifically — than their European conquerors. Even so, the conquerors looked down on those cultures and only saw the people as unsophisticated heathens. The Spaniards and other Europeans were blinded by their own self-importance and their thirst for gold, and were not sensitive enough or wise enough, to understand or appreciate the wisdom of the cultures they encountered and then conquered. Almost all of the wisdom of these advanced cultures was lost.

Past Lives

People are often curious about who they were in past lives and what they did. Although it may seem entertaining, there is a chance that digging back into past lives can negatively affect and even contaminate your learning process in this lifetime. Digging into past lifetimes can be an ego trip and can cause more harm than good. There is a good reason why the veil is shut when a person is born.

From a spiritual perspective, we have enough to handle by just focusing on the lessons we are learning in this lifetime.

Imagine that you were born into a family where, in a past life, a close relative murdered you. In your current lifetime, you have the opportunity to make peace and to get it right. However if you become consciously aware of your past lives, that knowledge might limit, affect or influence your patterns of interaction. By not knowing, you have a better chance to heal it.

The only time I look into a client's past lives is when I am being directed to do so by my intuition, guidance or spirit. We keep repeating patterns until we clear them, so if an issue is showing up in this lifetime, it may have originated in a previous one. When I'm tracking the energy during a healing or coaching session, I first look for the deepest root cause of the challenge, fear or destructive pattern in this lifetime. If I cannot find it in this lifetime, then I look deeper to see if it originated from a past life. In either case, I will keep going deeper and deeper until I energetically sense or see the event creating the challenge, and help my client to clear it.

Who you were in your past lives — in fact, who you were yesterday — is not as nearly as important as who you are today. Stay in the present and do your absolute best in each and every moment. That is more than enough.

Bodhisattva

Bodhisattva is a Sanskrit term that describes a human being with great compassion who has made a deep commitment to his own spiritual path, to helping others and to helping the Earth heal. A bodhisattva is not easily seduced by power, status or wealth. Unlike most other humans, bodhisattvas have graduated from the Earth plane, however they consciously chose to return to Earth to help, teach and serve others, rather than leave the Earth plane altogether and move on to other soul lessons.

* * *

The Final Teaching Story

There is a story about three old Greek monks, who were the last of their religious order. They were concerned because when they died, their order would be lost forever. So they sought out the advice of a very wise man. The man listened intently and then asked the monks to come back in three weeks.

When the monks returned, the wise man looked at all three of the monks, and then with deep reverence said, "One of you is the Messiah." That's all the wise man would say. As the monks left, each monk wondered if he was the Messiah, or not.

As the weeks passed, these monks transformed, becoming quieter, kinder, gentler, and more reflective, respectful, reverent and centered. There were times when each of their egos would puff up wondering if he was the Messiah. However just as fast, he became even more humble, wondering if he wasn't and one of the other monks was.

In the months that followed, the great love, respect and reverence these three monks had for each other grew more tangible. The pure positive respectful energy they radiated was inviting. Slowly at first, people started coming, and then more and more people were attracted to these monks. Some people came wanting to pray with the monks, while others wanted to join the order.

As a result of the great reverence and respect these three monks had for each other, the order was reborn, blossomed and flourished.

What would your life be like if you honored yourself and the Divinity within yourself this much? And what would the world be like if each person, family, organization, company and country treated themselves and each other with the same level of respect and reverence as these monks did?

Chapter 12
Points to Ponder & Take with You

We've covered a tremendous amount of information in these pages, so I'd like to leave you with some guideposts to assist you on your Earth adventure:

1. Mastering the internal struggle between your ego and personality on the one hand, and your soul or divine spirit on the other, is one of the greatest challenges and lessons of an evolving human being on Earth. Until you fully activate and align your will and your intention towards your spiritual essence and choose with all your mind, heart and soul to tame your ego and personality, there will always be a power struggle between these two opposing energies within you. This means that in each and every moment, you can choose to either follow your ego/personality's path or your soul's path.

2. You get to choose your lessons, your actions and reactions, and the path you wish to follow. If you are not happy with your choices, you can always choose again. You can choose to resist and suffer as much as you wish, and you can take as long as you like to learn your lessons. Or you can choose to take total responsibility, and surrender to fully embracing and learning your lessons. By the way, pain, resistance and suffering are optional. So choose wisely!

3. Another option you have is to completely avoid taking any responsibility for your choices by not making any choices at all. However, if you don't take full responsibility for yourself, other people and the situations you're in will make those choices for you. (Note: Not making a choice, however, is still a choice on your part!) Either way, you will reap the benefits or suffer the consequences of the choices you do or don't make. Hopefully, with time, you will become a lot more skilled at taking responsibility for yourself and making healthier choices.

4. Be *in* the world, but not of the world. Live life fully. Appreciate and fully embrace life, living, feelings, emotions, money, power, material possessions and your sexuality without allowing them to dominate, control or possess you. Avoid getting caught up in fear, anger, blame, shame, guilt or struggle. Do your best to remain calm, centered, peaceful, playful, authentic and present. Above all, never take things personally.

5. On a soul level, your progress is not measured by your short-term successes or failures, or how much material wealth you accumulate. What's far more important than winning, losing, status or material wealth is the way in which you live your life. This includes the way you motivate yourself to learn, risk, change, grow, expand, and how passionately you live your life with integrity. While you can't take any material wealth with you when you leave the Earth plane, you can and will take all that you have learned and experienced! This is called knowledge and wisdom.

6. You'll continue to attract and repeat the same patterns over and over again until you finally master them. Each time you face a lesson and make progress in your learning process, you will cycle back to a different aspect of that same lesson on higher and subtler levels. You will be retested to make sure you have truly mastered all aspects of your lesson. Once you have mastered your lesson, it will dissolve and will no longer challenge you. Then you will move on and attract other lessons.

7. Everyone is at a different place on his or her own unique path of learning for this lifetime. This makes it extremely challenging to judge others. We are each at different levels of soul growth, consciousness, awareness and experience. Hence, each of us is perfect in our own unique way. We are always exactly where we need to be, doing exactly what we need to be doing in this precise moment to learn our perfect lessons. Knowing and accepting this principle helps you to accept your lessons and experiences, and those of others.

8. Whenever you get triggered and react to something, you are being shown one of your unhealed wounds — an area that you need to pay attention to, focus on, change and heal. Everything is about you and not the other person. It can be very helpful to have a conscious, highly intuitive coach, mentor or teacher to help you identify what is really going on so you can pinpoint what is triggering you, identify why you are being triggered and find the best approach to heal the issue.

9. Most of us have a tendency to want to do what comes easily and naturally to us. We like to do what we are comfortable with, what we are good at and what brings us recognition. From an ego and personality level, this ensures that we continue to look good, play it safe, stay with where we are comfortable and stay in control. However, from a soul perspective, simply repeating skills and lessons we have already mastered does not support our continued soul growth and is a waste of our Earth time. Repeating experiences we've already mastered usually indicates that we are avoiding risking, learning, changing, growing, exploring, expanding and moving forward in this lifetime. This is especially true when we are coming off of a mastery lifetime and starting a practice lifetime. However, even though you may be extremely skilled in one area, it is important to pay attention when you experience your heart and soul calling you to do something very different. You might feel a strong pull to start a new business venture, career, hobby, life adventure or relationship that gives your heart great joy. This

can be similar to a mid-life crisis, when, without warning, someone chooses to leave the safety and security of a successful career and/or marriage in order to follow the calling of his or her heart and soul.

10. People tend to judge others and especially themselves as being imperfect, not good enough and undeserving. Often, the person we judge unmercifully, criticize the most and are by far the harshest critic of, is ourselves. The sooner we learn to stop judging and criticizing others and especially ourselves and learn to be kind, gentle, caring, sensitive, accepting, nurturing and compassionate to everyone including ourselves, the sooner we will be free to truly live our life!

11. Life is a journey — not a destination. The more you can accept your challenges and relax into your learning process while still appreciating and enjoying your journey, the more fun your journey will be. One of the greatest talents to have in life is to be able to laugh at yourself!

12. For many of us, one of our greatest lessons in life is to learn to ask for, and accept help and support from others. Although you have chosen your journey, your challenges and your lessons, you do not have to face these or go through this lifetime alone and unsupported. You are allowed to ask for and receive guidance, help, support and healing. It can be extremely helpful to have a conscious, highly intuitive healer, coach or teacher to help you to identify your challenges, lessons and your strengths. This support person can also assist you to determine the easiest, fastest, best solutions and path forward, in both your personal and professional life. Without the assistance of the healers, guides and teachers I've had along my journey, I would not be where I am today. Asking for and graciously accepting help, healing, support and guidance, while still taking full personal responsibility for yourself, will greatly speed and ease your journey.

Identifying and clearing your core issues, resolving your challenges and learning your life lessons are not an easy task to do on your own. If it were, you would have already accomplished it by now. Please know that you are not alone and you do not have to face the challenges of your Earth journey on your own. You can ask for and receive guidance, help and support!

Dear Reader,

Thank you for reading this book!

May you greatly benefit from this information!

Namaste, All My Relations, Many Blessings, Om Shanti

Michael Bradford

Connect with Michael

Give Michael your feedback! How did you like this book? What realizations did you have as you were reading this book? What question do you have? What additional information would you like? Michael appreciates hearing from you and receiving your questions, comments, feedback and insights.

Would you please do Michael a huge favor? Could you please give your positive feedback on the site where you purchased this book? This is extremely important as it will help others to become aware of the help and support the information in this book provides. Thank you.

Would you like to learn from Michael? Are you interested in developing your healing ability and your intuition, or becoming an apprentice?

Let Michael know what other subjects, topics and information you'd like to learn about. Are you interested in learning more about your intuition, healing, universal laws, the Law of Attraction, creative visualization, affirmations, manifestation and intention? What other programs would you like Michael to create to support you on your journey?

Michael has dedicated his life to assisting, guiding and supporting people who are on this Earth journey. Should you wish Michael's guidance, help and support with your personal or business challenges please contact him.

You can ask for and receive guidance, help and support!

For Coaching, Mentoring, Business and Consulting clients, Michael offers a FREE 20 minute consultation to explore how Michael can support you.

FREE — Newsletter & Extra Bonus Materials

When you sign up for Michael's FREE newsletter you'll get FREE Additional Bonus Materials including discount coupons.

FREE — Intuition Training Program

One of the skills Michael is most interested in and committed to teaching is Intuition Training. He is currently writing a book and designing a training program that will explain what Intuition is and teach you how to develop your Intuition.

If you would like to be part of the core group, which asks Michael questions and gives him feedback, he would be more than happy to help you develop your intuition.

This program will be FREE to the core group. Please contact him if you are interested.

FREE — Personal Training & Apprenticeship Opportunities With Michael

This Program is Free for Active Participants through December 31, 2019. Contact Michael for details.

Private Healing, Coaching & Mentoring Sessions And Trainings

Private Sessions
Coaching and Mentoring
Life-Changing Weekend Workshops
Training Programs:
Healer Training Program
Intuition Training Program
Apprenticeship Program
Mystery School
Joint Venture Opportunities
Affiliate Program Available

Book Michael

Book Michael for talks, workshops and trainings in person or online. Should you wish to sponsor Michael in your area, please call or send him an email.

Michael Bradford's Contact Information

Phone: 760-844-2778 (USA)

Web: www.MichaelBradford.com

Email: Michael@MichaelBradford.com

FaceBook: www.facebook.com/MichaelBradfordGlobal

LinkedIn: www.linkedin.com/in/michaeledwardbradford

Skype: Michael.Bradford.Global

YouTube: www.youtube/c/MichaelEdwardBradford

About The Author — Michael Bradford

Michael Bradford is an international intuitive energy healer, business coach, author and spiritual teacher with extensive expertise in the areas of health, healing, personal excellence, spiritual growth, entrepreneurship, success and wealth creation. He has a Masters Degree in International Management and advanced training in Intuition, NLP, Hypnosis, Reiki, Energy Medicine, Reading Energy Patterns and many other specialties.

Throughout his travels, he has shared healing experiences with Native American Medicine People, Canadian Medicine People, an Eskimo healer, Peruvian shamans, psychic surgeons from the Philippines, the Maoris and many hundreds of other therapists, healers, psychics, shamans and medical professionals. He has assisted countless medical and healing practitioners, including chiropractors, holistic medical doctors, psychiatrists and therapists, to help heal their patients.

Using his unique, cutting-edge, multidimensional methods, Michael has helped thousands of clients in over thirty countries to break free of their limitations, balance karma and become more successful. They've gained greater access to their intuition, sped up their healing process, accelerated their spiritual growth, gained clarity, improved relationships, attracted greater success and increased their finances. Michael offers private sessions, coaching, mentoring and in-depth workshops on personal breakthrough, financial success and intuition training. He is also available for conferences, keynote speeches, summits and joint ventures.